CHANGING DIRECTIONS
WITHOUT
LOSING YOUR WAY

OTHER BOOKS BY
PAUL AND SARAH EDWARDS

The Practical Dreamer's Handbook

The Best Home Businesses for the 21st Century

Cool Careers for Dummies (WITH MARTY NEMKO)

Home-Based Businesses for Dummies (WITH PETER ECONOMY)

Home Businesses You Can Buy (WITH WALTER ZOOI)

Finding Your Perfect Work

Getting Business to Come to You (WITH LAURA CLAMPITT DOUGLAS)

Making Money in Cyberspace (WITH LINDA ROHRBOUGH)

Making Money with Your Computer at Home

Secrets of Self-Employment

Teaming Up (WITH RICK BENZEL)

Working from Home

CHANGING DIRECTIONS
WITHOUT
LOSING YOUR WAY

Managing the Six Stages
of Change at Work
and in Life

PAUL AND SARAH EDWARDS

JEREMY P. TARCHER • PUTNAM
a member of Penguin Putnam Inc.
New York

Most Tarcher/Putnam books are available at special quantity discounts for bulk
purchase for sales promotions, premiums, fund-raising, and educational needs.
Special books or book excerpts also can be created to fit specific needs. For details,
write Putnam Special Markets, 375 Hudson Street, New York, NY 10014.

Jeremy P. Tarcher/Putnam
a member of
Penguin Putnam Inc.
375 Hudson Street
New York, NY 10014
www.penguinputnam.com

Library of Congress Cataloging-in-Publication Data
Edwards, Paul, date.
Changing directions without losing your way : managing the six stages of
change at work and in life / Paul and Sarah Edwards.
p.   cm.
Includes index.
ISBN 1-58542-076-X
1. Vocational guidance—United States.   2. Self-realization—United States.
3. Vocational interests—United States.   4. Professions—United States.
I. Edwards, Sarah (Sarah A.)   II. Title

HF5382.5U5 E327   2000   00-064781
158.1—dc21

Printed in the United States of America

1   3   5   7   9   10   8   6   4   2

BOOK DESIGN BY DEBORAH KERNER

Acknowledgments

We want to thank all those who have participated in our Changing Directions seminars and others we interviewed who so willingly shared their experiences with us and allowed us to share them with our readers. Thanks, too, to Justen McCormack for her day-to-day assistance in getting this book ready for publication and, of course, many thanks to the staff of Tarcher/Putnam with whom we have worked for so many years.

Contents

CHANGING DIRECTIONS
WITHOUT
LOSING YOUR WAY

CHANGING DIRECTIONS
WITHOUT
LOSING YOUR WAY

Our natures lie in motion,
without which we die.

— PASCAL

Introduction:
The Essential Tools for Change

Hurrah! Voilà! Oh, boy! Today you're excited, elated, exhilarated, relieved about all the possibilities for what could be. Oh, no! Drat! Damn! The next day you're distressed, depressed, discouraged, even panicked. Your life is about to take a dramatic turn. Or maybe it already has. Things will probably never be quite the same, but a whole new life is about to begin . . . you hope. Some days you convince yourself you won't really need to change all that much after all. Life won't have to be all that different. But, in your heart you know it already is changing and will continue to change at an alarming rate.

Sound familiar? Most of us know this emotional roller coaster all too well. It's called change, and it's rushing through our lives like a river that's overflowing its banks. Whether it's desired, sought after, and eagerly awaited or forced upon us with dread, change has become the norm, and it's filling our lives with turmoil. For better or worse, an onslaught of unexpected and, for many, disappointing developments along with a wealth of demanding new opportunities is turning the way we live and work upside down.

Seemingly, it can happen with virtually no warning. Suddenly, you're struggling to find your footing. Maybe you've walked away from a thriving career to pursue a long-awaited goal, or perhaps that once-thriving career has left you scrambling for survival. Whatever the details, like most of us, you sense big changes swirling around you and know they can knock you off your feet, sweep you away, or pull you under and drown your dreams. Of course, you'd prefer to think, they can carry you to a better life you've been dreaming of, or one even better than you could have imagined, because you know that's possible, too.

How do we ride these currents of change that are surging through us and around us without losing our way? That's the skill of the new century, one we all must master, and the subject of this book.

The Message Is:
You Can't Stop the River

For the past two decades, we've seen hundreds of thousands of people take on the life-altering changes today's technology-packed world has been presenting them. We've seen some flounder, but we've seen far more use the changes around them to craft new and better ways of living and working that past generations could never have thought possible. Through our seminars and books, we've played a role in helping tens of thousands of them make such changes.

People are changing directions, for a variety of reasons. They may have heard stories like the one we heard when, because of managed health care, our podiatrist told us he was closing his practice to enroll in nursing school. And they fear similar changes could be under way in their fields. Or they may have heard one-too-many times that another twenty-five-year-old is well on the way to becoming a millionaire, and they want to pursue fame and fortune from their own great ideas. Perhaps their neighbor has moved his family and business to the mountains of Montana, and they, too, want to live somewhere idyllic.

Some people may have been downsized for the fourth time and swear that will never happen again. Or, they dread another morning of taking their toddlers to day care before dawn, so they're ready to start a home business where they can spend more time with their kids. They may have already started a business and it isn't what they hoped, so they're wanting to find something new that will. Or maybe, they just can't take another day like yesterday but don't know what else to do.

In other words, millions of other men and women have realized a river of change is surging through their lives and they've got to change directions. Since you're reading this book, chances are there's a powerful current of change moving through your life, too. You may not know quite where you're headed or just how you're going to get there, but you know you can't stop the river, whether you want to or not.

The Problem Is:
There Are No More Branches to Hang on To

Some of us thrive on change, but many of us don't. Even *successful* people can lose their way as the landscape of their lives and careers shifts beneath their feet and changes before their eyes. A prominent media personality who was profiled posthumously in the *Los Angeles Times Magazine,* for example, had reached the apex of his career when changes in the world of media cut him out of both his syndicated radio and television shows. His despair in trying to find his way back to the prominence he'd enjoyed led first to bankruptcy, then to deteriorating health and, ultimately, to an untimely death at the age of fifty-seven.

Not long after this article appeared, *The New York Times* reported on how celebrated doctors and experienced nurses at the peak of their careers are finding themselves jobless, as the institutions to which they brought prestige have made such stature secondary to their bottom lines.

Virtually, every field we profiled in *The Best Home Businesses for the 21st Century,* from multimedia production and financial planning to micro-farming and family day care, are undergoing similar ego and life-altering changes. But these very changes are also creating the new millionaires from among the most ambitious and well positioned among us, and simpler, more satisfying lives for those who need a change of pace and an escape from the rat race. Increasing numbers of us are deciding we want to change how we live, what we do, and where we do it. The problem is, most of us still aren't all that adept at white-water rafting, but that's what's required to navigate the tumultuous changes sweeping through our lives.

Once upon a time, aside from personal tragedies or national disasters, most changes drifted lazily through our lives. Much like the process of growing up and growing older, we hardly noticed them in the day-to-day mirror of life. Except for highly anticipated transitions, such as graduating from school, leaving home, getting married, and starting a family, there were few sharp turns over the course of our lives, and the handling of the curves was challenge enough.

Now, both internal and external changes are turning our lives into a series of white-water rapids along a course of nonstop sharp turns. In our hearts, we've grown restless and dissatisfied. We want to move on, but the currents within and around us are so rapid and tumultuous, we fear we'll drown if we don't hold on. So, often we get stuck in the mud as we try to hold tightly to the very life we want and need to change. Or we just give up and allow the current to carry us away, careening over the rapids, bouncing from shore to shore, with our eye's closed, fingers crossed, and a prayer on our breath.

Yet increasingly, even the seemingly safe paths we've chosen and prepared ourselves for are leading us over a cliff or slamming us into an abrupt dead end. Over and over again, we're having to turn on a dime, retreat, regroup, and head in some new direction. The result is a life of what we call "—ession" sessions. We suffer from bouts of:

"Obsession"—worrying, plotting, and planning, in an endless loop of analysis paralysis over how we can stem the tides and take control of our lives.

"Repression"—denying what we truly want while exhausting ourselves busily to turn the lemons in our lives into lemonade.

"Depression"—giving up all sense of our power to affect the course of our lives and succumbing to our greatest fears and doubts.

But, as we realize that we can't hold on to what has been, that there are no more safe branches but plenty of logjams to get tangled up in, some of us are beginning to ask, why not take the more unconventional paths we'd really rather take, anyway? Could they be any less treacherous or risky? If we were following the currents in our hearts instead of trying to hold on to the sides of life, could we go with the flow without going under?

Without the right tools the answer is "no." We've all seen people flounder in the rapids of their dreams. Your dreams may already have been dashed on the rocks of change at least once. But with the right tools, the answer is "yes." And that's what this book is about. It provides tools vital for making whatever changes you're wanting or needing to make, be they dramatic alterations or mere course corrections, all the while keeping your head above water so you can see where you're headed and steer to a desired destination.

The Solution Is: Seven Essential Tools for Navigating the Waters of Change

No one would go white-water rafting without the proper gear and other resources. Change, too, requires that we stock up on the proper travel gear. We need a map of the territory. We need a compass to tell us where we're headed. We need perspective to assess where we are and a strategy for getting where we want to go. We need traveling companions we can turn to along the way, and, finally, we need adequate fuel to get there. These are the tools you'll find in this book.

A MAP OF THE TERRITORY:
THE SIX STAGES OF CHANGE

Change is by nature unpredictable, but the stages we go through in undertaking it are quite predictable. So, while you may not know where you're headed in the midst of change and thus feel lost, if you understand the process of change, you need never be lost. We have identified six distinct stages in the process of changing directions, and recognizing them enables you to always know where you are, what you need to do, and where you're headed next.

As long as your energy is moving forward in a desired direction, these stages of change can be exhilarating and empowering, even enjoyable. But if for any reason you get stuck in a particular stage or are unable to take the change in a desired direction, it can become difficult, unpleasant, and even unbearable. The resulting emotional and practical logjams can clog your life and affect your well-being and even your health.

So, we've written the book much like a workbook or guide to facilitate your journey through the six stages of changing directions. There is a chapter for each of the six stages that includes specific tasks you must complete, questions you should ask, and the challenges and logjams you might expect to meet. You'll also find plenty of specific examples and practical guidance for how to move through each stage as quickly and easily as possible.

The first stage, outlined in chapter one, *Facing a New Reality: Recognizing It's Time to Move On*, involves accepting that you can't change until you accept that you must change and decide to take charge of changing your life. Chapter two, *Saying Goodbye to Where You've Been: Releasing the Past*, addresses the second stage of change—letting go of what has been so you can free up the time and energy to create a new future. Chapter three, *Finding Your Way: The Inner Compass*, is actually about one of the other key tools you'll need to change—finding a deep inner sense or conviction about who we are, regardless of our external circumstances.

Chapter four, *Saying Hello to Where You're Going: Embracing the Future*, is about the fourth stage of change, which requires that you focus in a specific new direction and make a commitment to a course of action. While each stage of change has its own challenges, we've found that people have more difficulty getting through this stage than any other. So, in this chapter, we provide a series of tools we've developed over the past twenty years for helping you find a match between your desires and talents on the one hand, and the realities of your life, on the other.

Chapter five, *Discovering How to Get There from Here: Developing a Strategy*, is about the fifth stage of changing directions, a plan for how you'll coordinate and draw upon all your available resources to make the changes you desire. It deals with the tough issues, like finding the money, making the time, and having the energy to implement the changes you're seeking to make.

Chapter six, *Putting the Show on the Road: Experimenting, Initiating, and Following Through*, is about actually making the change you want to make, which is the sixth stage. This involves handling whatever challenges arise and juggling life as it has been, while you create your new life.

Even if you are eager to change, you may unconsciously resist moving through some of these stages. Most people do. So, in each chapter you'll find insights into how you can unknowingly sabotage your own efforts to make the very changes you want to make. In a section called **"Hung Up?"** you'll find tools for untangling your hang-ups with change. Also, since navigating these stages is inevitably an emotional experience, the appendix, *A Guide to Handling the Emotions of Change*, provides tools for transforming even the most common negative feelings we all experience when trying to change our lives into positive forces in order to help us make the changes we're seeking.

AN INNER COMPASS:
CHARTING YOUR COURSE

In trying to change directions, it's easy to get lost in the options. We may see the future as a barren desert with no appealing choices or as a tropical jungle of far too many options from which to choose. Not knowing in what direction to go, we may hop on the bandwagon of whatever's "hot" at the moment, only to end up having to change directions again when what's "hot" cools or doesn't work out for us. Therefore, one of the most important tools for changing directions without losing your way is a clear sense of who you are as a person. When you know who you are, you can never really be lost. The knowledge of your true self can always be an "inner compass," directing you toward the most desirable path in your life.

Your inner compass can both point you in the right direction and let you know when you're off course. Without it, you're forever susceptible to confusion, fear, and self-doubt, but with it as your guide, you can find an unshakable sense of confidence and courage.

Studies of identical twins separated at birth conducted at California State University at Fullerton suggest that satisfaction at work is closely correlated with intrinsic rewards that are genetically determined. So if we want to be happy with our careers, we should pay close attention to our inner yearnings.

A GETAWAY:
GAINING NEEDED PERSPECTIVE

It's hard to see the future when you're blinded by the practicalities of the present. Finding your way to a new life requires perspective. So, using this book will be infinitely easier if you don't try to squeeze reading it into the crevices of the myriad of details and complexities of your current life. As Frances Mayes writes in *Under the Tuscany Sun*, ". . . to seek change probably always is related to the desire to enlarge the psychic place one lives in." Thus, providing yourself with a chance to get away from your existing circumstances for a period of time is another key tool for change.

In fact, this book began as a retreat called *Get Away for a Change* which we developed for professionals and small business owners and which we offer in our home in the Los Padres National Forest of California. Physically removed from all reminders of their past and present, participants in these retreats are able to see their desired future with a new clarity and creativity. Therefore, we recommend that you treat this book itself as a retreat. Set aside as much time away from your normal routine as you possibly can in order to read it and work through the processes suggested in each chapter.

Ideally, you might take a week or more to get away to a quiet, natural setting where you can relax, renew your energy, and reach into the depths of your creativity. Of course, if you're rolling on the floor laughing at that suggestion, we understand. Not everyone can get away for a long period of time, so do what you can to set aside brief weekend, day-long, morning, afternoon, or evening retreats in some quiet, nearby, relaxing place. In many cases, you may want and need to get away repeatedly, for whatever period of time you can, over several months, as you work your way through each of the stages of taking your life in a new direction.

As in physics, so in life, the antidote to pressure is space. To find creative solutions and new options, we need to escape the pressures of daily demands and find a place where we can let our imagination out of its box of scheduled routines and allow it to soar.

A CHANGE JOURNAL:
REFLECTING ON THE JOURNEY

Without reflection there can be no inspiration. Unless you can reflect upon your circumstances and what your inner compass is guiding you to do, you will forever be grasping at straws and wondering why you either remain stuck in a rut or out of control. One of the most important reasons for getting away from the clatter and clutter of your existing life is so you can reflect upon what is in your heart and gain still greater perspective on how to harmonize your own needs with the realities of your life situation.

You'll find many invitations for reflection in special italic text sections throughout each chapter, as well as in CLOSING REFLECTIONS at the end of each chapter. These are opportunities for you to close the book and reflect upon the changing directions in your life. We recommend taking ample time for each reflection process. We also suggest that you create your own Change Journal, be it on paper or in your computer, where you can take notes, explore, summarize, or draw out your reflections. Putting your reflections in writing or graphic images can be a powerful first step toward materializing a new future. It turns your ideas and dreams and imaginations into tangible, visible manifestations for you to review, reconsider, and reflect upon further.

A North Dakota State University study found that writing about stressful experiences can relieve tension, boost the immune system, and reduce the physical symptoms of stress.

TRAVELING COMPANIONS:
GETTING SUPPORT

Those who attend our *Get Away for a Change* workshops tell us that one of the most valuable tools for making changes in their lives has been sharing their experiences and reflections with others in the workshops and the ongoing group teleconferences that follow. Therefore, this book itself is set up much like one of our workshops in that you will be meeting specific people who, like yourself, are in the process of changing directions. While their names and circumstances have been changed to protect their privacy, these are real individuals, or occasionally composites of individuals, who have agreed to share their experiences as you go through the same processes they have gone through.

In addition to benefiting from the presence of the individuals in this book, you are invited to consider reading it with a partner and doing the processes together, discussing your reflections with one another, and perhaps even getting away for a brief retreat together. You might want to invite a group of like-minded friends and colleagues to get together weekly to read this book, much as in a book club. The goal would, of course, be much more than just reading the book, however. It would be to support one another in navigating your own white-water rapids. The CLOSING REFLECTIONS at the end of each chapter can serve as a launching pad for group discussion.

Our environment and personal habits determine 70 percent of how healthy we are, according to Centers for Disease Control and Prevention.

FUEL: Building Energy and Stamina

Remember, to change directions, you've got to get going and keep moving. That means you have to have the energy to propel yourself from where you are to where you want to go, even when you're navigating the rapids or having to go against a current that isn't taking you in the right direction. Yet change is stressful for most people, and this stress can put a drag on your energy. It can wear you down and tire you out. Fortunately, though, there are specific things you can do easily to keep your energy up and flowing. These things fuel your body; yet it's easy to get busy and forget to stay fueled up. But taking the time to make sure you're doing the following four simple things consistently each day will help you maintain yourself in a vigorous and high state of energy:

Breathing. Regular deep and rhythmic breathing enables you to keep refreshed physically and mentally, and provides you with the fuel to breath through the problems and challenges of change. It's the one autonomic body function we can consciously regulate. So to be sure you're getting the oxygen you need to keep moving, take note of your breathing patterns. If you find you're short of breath or sighing a lot, your body is signally you that you're holding your breath and need to focus on taking in deeper, longer breaths.

Water. Our bodies need ample water every day to keep the right electrolyte balance. To calculate how much you should be drinking, divide your body weight in half. That's the number of ounces you should be drinking, at a minimum. So if you weigh 120 pounds, you need to drink 60 ounces of water a day. If you drink coffee, alcohol, or soda, which deplete electrolytes, you'll need to drink even more water to function optimally. So, don't deprive yourself. Don't try to run on empty. Build drinking plenty into each day.

Exercise. Exercise literally gets you moving. It gives all your organs and bodily functions the workout they need to get tuned up to operate effectively. We go along with the experts who recommend a minimum of twenty minutes each day of physical exercise.

Alkaline Foods. The body works best when it's in an alkaline state. So, if you eat foods high in acid like red meat, salty snacks, and sugary desserts that create an acidic buildup in your body, this will drain your energy. But an alkaline diet with lots of fresh fruits and vegetable has just the opposite effect. It keeps you healthy, nourished, and energized.

Doing these four simple things can have more impact on your ability to change than just about anything else you can do. They are well worth the investment. To do otherwise is like trying to undertake your journey in a leaky boat. So, throughout the book, you'll find sections called TURBO FUEL, which include some tips on how to make sure you're drinking plenty of water, breathing deeply, exercising regularly, and eating hearty alkaline foods. Should you find yourself resisting fueling up in these four ways at any stage in the change process, we would invite you to reflect on why you would want to handicap your journey. It could provide some valuable insights into what's hanging you up.

CLOSING REFLECTION: Where Are You Now?

What stage are you in at this process of changing directions? Use the following list below to review your progress. Based on your current and past experience, is there any particular stage where you're likely to get stuck? How do you feel about your progress up to this point? How would you describe your journey?

THE SIX STAGES OF CHANGING DIRECTIONS

1. Facing Reality: Recognizing It's Time to Move On
2. Saying Goodbye to Where You've Been: Releasing the Past
3. Finding Your Way: Your Inner Compass
4. Saying Hello to Where You're Going: Embracing the Future
5. Discovering How to Get There from Here: Developing a Strategy
6. Putting Your Show on the Road: Experimenting, Initiating, and Following Through

Learning to change directions quickly, easily, and with confidence is much like learning to play golf or doing public speaking: you can only master it by doing it yourself. It's like being pregnant; you can't delegate the delivery. No one else can do it for you. But you don't have to be alone in doing it. You can get assistance and support. You can have company along the way. But changing directions is a process we each must go through personally.

Thus, as you proceed through this book, you will be invited to actually work your way through each of the six stages. As you do, you'll most likely confront painful or unpleasant aspects of your life that you may not have been unaware of. But you will also most likely stumble over buried treasures you'd long forgotten or possibly never realized you possessed, along with new aspects of yourself and possible futures you've only dreamed of that will delight and inspire you. At times, you may feel lost or discouraged. But if you keep moving through the processes, you'll undoubtedly discover, as our workshop participants have, that within the changes you face lie the magic and wonder of a new and better future.

FACING A NEW REALITY: RECOGNIZING IT'S TIME TO MOVE ON

Change is the rock in everyone's shoe . . . and some people limp.
—REG MURPHY, CEO, *NATIONAL GEOGRAPHIC*

Sometimes, it's like a rear-end collision—sudden and completely unexpected. Mark, for example, had been looking forward to lunch with his division head, who was flying in from Chicago for the meeting. The Christmas holidays were approaching. Mark had slipped in some last-minute shopping at the department store next to the restaurant where they were to meet. The mall was bustling with holiday cheer that was all the more festive that day because there was already a coat of fresh snow on the streets. In the distance, the Rocky Mountains were glistening in the sunlight of a sky-blue day.

The lunch began on a pleasant note. In the back of his mind, Mark was half expecting that a promotion was in the offing. His last performance evaluation had been excellent, and over the past year several of his ideas had been successfully implemented throughout the region. Midway through the entrée, however, the conversation took on a somber note, and Mark felt a sharp twinge of fear grip his chest. He shook it off. "Don't be silly," he reassured himself silently, as he tried to focus on his superior's increasingly grave remarks about the future of the company. "Relax, you've been with this company for over ten years. Your future here is secure," he kept reminding himself.

Then, in less than the time it took for Mark to lift the next bite of his lemon pepper chicken to his mouth, he got the message. The company was downsizing. The branch office would be closing January 1. Mark would be let go at the close of business that day!

Other times, it's more like running out of gas—gradual and accompanied with ample warning signs we may or may not heed. Clarissa, for example, had been worried about the decline in her referral business for several months. But, she kept telling herself, all businesses go through seasonal slumps. "I'll just boost my marketing and things will pick up again," she concluded with the confidence ten years of being in your own successful business can bring. But, as the months passed, things didn't pick up. In fact, they had declined further.

Clarissa had to let one of her two employees go, then the other. Then she moved her office home. "Why pay all that rent?" she rationalized. Anyway, she enjoyed working from home. But by the end of year, Clarissa realized the market for her business had dried up. People just didn't need what she was offering any longer. She was going to have to do something else for a living.

At first, Denise thought her increasing fatigue was simply the remnants of a bad case of the flu. But sick days turned into a leave of absence as doctors searched in vain to find the cause of her growing malaise. At last, she learned she had a rare systemic infection that would require many months of recovery. But even then, Denise assumed that within time, she'd be able to return to her lifelong career as a forest ranger. That was not to be. Gradually, she realized that the disease had taken a toll on her body that would prevent her from ever resuming the level of physical exertion and activity her chosen career demanded. She would have to change not only her career but also her lifestyle.

Often, as with Mark, Clarissa, and Denise, the realization that we must change directions is not of our own choosing. But equally as often these days, it is. Vickie, for example, had worked as an editor for a national newspaper for twenty-two years. But, while she loved writing, over the years her job had changed. Getting out of bed on Monday mornings was increasingly difficult for her. Her mind kept wandering to other kinds of articles she'd like to be writing. But, she kept reminding herself, she had a job thousands of starving writers could only dream of. It provided money, prestige, security, and the opportunity to not only earn a living doing what she loved, but to have tens of thousands of people read her work every day! What more could she want? One morning, however, Vickie finally realized that by the time she pulled into her assigned parking space for work each morning, "I was furious." She could no longer ignore deny it. She needed to make a change.

So did Donald. He was vice president of marketing for one of the nation's largest advertising agencies. The money was great! But he was increasingly disturbed. He was devoting his career to promoting a growing list of products he didn't believe in: cigarettes, alcohol, gas-guzzling automobiles, and artery-clogging junk food. Still, he didn't see any alternatives. He had a family. They had become accustomed to a certain lifestyle and a high standard of living. Any similar-paying marketing position he entertained presented the same problems. So he stayed on with the company until suddenly one day, right in the middle of a presentation to a client, he simply couldn't continue talking. He excused himself and tried to regain his composure to go on. But he could not. He realized at that moment, he had to make a change.

Susan was working as a well-paid media manager and policy advisor for a high-profile politician when both her parents passed away and left her some money. This provided her with the opportunity to do something she'd been wanting to do for a long time: quit her job and take a year off to go back to school to study journalism and fulfill her longtime dream of writing a novel. At the end of that year, however, in the midst of a recession and unable to find a job, Susan's life took an unexpected downward spiral. Five years later, she found herself an alcoholic, having DT's, homeless, and in a county hospital with an IV in her arm, surrounded by people who were literally dying of liver failure. She had hit bottom. "I said to myself, 'This isn't right. I'll never take another drink.'" And thus began a three-year journey to rebuild the foundation of her life.

Whether it's sudden or gradual, chosen, or inflicted upon us, the moment of truth comes when we know we must change.

Has that moment come in your life? When did you know, or first suspect, it was time to change directions?

The Task Is:
Accepting That Something
Significant Is Happening

When it's time for a change, the sooner you get to the message the better. Too often, like Susan, life has to get pretty awful before we wake up to the fact that things can't remain the same. The longer it takes us to realize that a change is coming, the more of a sudden, jolting, wrenching sharp turn it will be. But, if we see what's coming well before it's upon us, we can avoid the sharp turns and take change on the curves.

TURNING SHARP TURNS INTO CURVES

A drama was unfolding before us. When we first interviewed Annette, she was writing a subscription newsletter for businesses featuring upcoming events in her community. But the newsletter was barely breaking even. She got the message immediately. This business idea was a good one but it wasn't working. The information she was providing, although valuable, wasn't sufficiently profitable to her subscribers to entice them to pay subscription rates that would cover her rising costs of printing and mailing the newsletter.

Quick to respond, Annette was about to close her business when she had a hunch. More businesses were using fax machines. What if she provided her newsletter via fax instead of in print? This would eliminate her printing costs and dramatically reduce her mailing costs. She tested this concept, and it was a winner. Not only did the number of subscriptions jump, but because the information was more timely, she also was able to raise subscription prices. Suddenly, her venture was not only breaking even but providing an excellent income.

People in other communities were impressed with Annette's results and were soon asking how they might start such a service. Again, quick to pick up on what was happening, she decided to package her business as a franchise. That aspect of her business was going equally well, when she got another hunch. The Internet would soon make this service all the easier to provide. But, in surveying the situation, she realized that, on the Internet, services like hers might be offered for free! Whoops! She realized that if she didn't act quickly, she would be faced with having to make a really sharp turn, and her business was moving too fast to make an about-face. A much larger company however, with the capital to launch a large, national advertising-supported site might find acquiring her company an asset to getting their own site off the ground quickly. Sure enough. Within no time, Annette was able to sell her business for enough money to give her ample time to decide what she wanted to do next with her life.

Most people hearing about Annette's success say, "Boy, was she lucky! She got out just in time." We don't think it was luck. It was Annette's ability to read the signs of change, heed their messages, and believe they were important enough to take immediate action on. To avoid sharp turns and meet change on the curves, we've got to wake up to what's going on around us. We have to stay open to what's happening and how we feel about ourselves and our lives. And, if possible, take action on what's coming around before it happens.

Once whatever's coming arrives, we're in the position of having to react to it, so we start out one step behind. We are in the position of having to catch up. But, if we pick up quickly on what's developing and take the initiative immediately, we can participate in the opportunities change brings, instead of cleaning up the messes it makes. The quicker we can recognize and accept the need for change, the more likely we can take action to be ahead of the curve.

READ THE SIGNS: THEY'RE THERE

There are always signs. Of course, it's common to hear people say, "I didn't see it coming. It just came out of the blue." But that doesn't mean there weren't any signs. Even those who don't see the changes coming that are about to knock them over will often comment upon reflection after the fact, "I should have seen it coming." In situations other than random acts of nature, there are almost always telltale foreshadowings of things to come. Annette sensed them; Mark didn't. Upon reflection on the months leading up to his boss's trip from Chicago, though, Mark realized there had been some writing on the wall. Albeit faded, there were readable signs that his company was in trouble, and changes were in the air. He just hadn't been paying attention.

Is it time for you to wake up?

Let's face it; most of us would prefer peace and safety to risk and tumult. Even if you don't like your life the way it is, at least it's familiar. But change changes all that. Change upsets the apple cart, even when it's change for the better. Change shakes up our routines and tests the limits of our beliefs. Past problems that we've carefully tucked away, in the deep storage of our minds, may come tumbling out in the midst of change. So sometimes, it seems easier to look the other way and overlook signals that would alert us to what's coming around the corner.

But if we feel safe enough to look at the evidence of change, we can stand on the hillside of our lives, survey the vistas around us, and see what's really happening out there. With confidence, we can foresee and contemplate threats to our security and well-being.

TURBO FUEL: To Rebuild Your Confidence

Build Your History of Success. Confidence is built upon a history of success. To build your confidence so you can welcome the signs of change, use your

Change Journal to recall six times in your life when you saw change coming and did something about it which turned out well.

I.e., "I had been working for the same government agency for about five years when I got a great job offer with an outside subcontractor. This job paid considerably more than I was making and gave me a lot more responsibility and freedom to work creatively. Also, there had been talk of an impending RIF (reduction in force) within our agency. So, finding a new position seemed like a good idea.

Boy, did I want this job. Visions of glory were dancing in my head. I was going in for my final interview. Word was out that I was their first choice. All I had to do was show up and sign on the dotted line. But, I kept having a nagging feeling of impending doom. And I kept putting off the meeting. Finally, I decided to re-evaluate my situation. Was this really my best career move? I let go of all my illusions of grandeur and took a serious look at my hesitancy. Well, truth was, there had been some scuttlebutt circulating that a lot of government agencies were pulling back on their subcontracted functions. What if that happened?

Well, I decided to pass on the job, and that's exactly what happened. Within less than a year, the company I would have been working for was out of business. Meanwhile, I applied for a transfer to another department with the agency where I worked which was expanding in response to new legislation. My old department was RIF'ed, but my career was secure. I think of this often when I'm doubtful about changes I need to be making.

We can't let fear of the unknown, of making the wrong decision or repeating past mistakes paralyze our judgment. We need to see and read the signs of change taking place within ourselves and in the world around us.

Internal Signs You Need to Make a Change

Sometimes, there are no external reasons for us to change. In fact, our circumstances may seem ideal to others or even be what we thought we wanted. Others may be pressing us to continue on as we are and offering enticing incentives. But, what we want and need to do may be changing, and as we change we must make changes. Check any of these signals of needing to change that apply to you.

____ Not wanting to get out of bed in the morning

____ Difficulty motivating yourself to do routine tasks

____ Losing interest in things that once engaged you

____ Nagging doubts about yourself and the course of your life

____ Feeling less self-confidence

____ Worrying about how you'll keep things together

____ Wishing you were someone else

____ Frequent bad dreams and nightmares

____ Increasing strife at home that you might be causing or contributing to

____ Feeling bored and disinterested

____ Feeling in a rut and restless

____ Feeling mildly depressed for days on end

____ Overeating or using alcohol and drugs to feel better or to escape

____ Feeling chronically tired, de-energized, and listless

____ Losing a sense of enthusiasm for life

____ Getting a mild or serious illness

____ Getting frequent headaches, stomach upset, other aches and pains

____ Difficulty sleeping, oversleeping

____ Consistently being irritable, complaining nagging, bitching

____ Feeling unfulfilled from your work—that you're not making a difference or impact that's important to you

____ Feeling annoyed, angry, resentful, blaming

External Signs of Change

Being able to foresee and recognize changes that could threaten your future is key to being able to change directions successfully. Here are a variety of signs that there are changes under way which you need to take note of, because they can and will affect you. Check any that apply to you:

____ You're working longer and harder but still losing ground

____ New technology being used that's rumored to possibly make your role or industry obsolete or to drastically alter it

____ When something is happening in your field that makes you shake your head in disbelief, surprise, discomfort

____ Layoffs or hiring freezes in your or other companies in your industry

____ People start using other products and services as substitutes for what you offer: i.e., people turning to chiropractors instead of going to a traditional medical doctor

____ Others leaving your field or being more closed-mouth and competitive

____ There's talk on the grapevine about re-engineering or reorganizing

____ Earnings, sales, stock, or number of customers are dropping

____ New legislation that is pending or adopted that eliminates the need for what you do or instituting unviable regulations

____ Anomalies and contradictions begin occurring in your field or your life. As Seena Sharp of Sharp Information says, "Anomalies are rarely anomalies."

____ When others in your field start to combine their work with other skills and interests acupuncturists and psychologists doing pet bereavement therapy or professional coaching

____ Growing number of obstacles to doing what once came easily

____ Your manager suggests you update your skills

Heed the Signs: They Matter

It's not enough to simply see the signs. We also have to get the message. Change can consume and overwhelm us, so it's tempting to pretend everything is just fine, even though there are definite challenges we should be assessing and attending to.

Mike was an elected county commissioner in a major metropolitan area. His schedule was jam-packed from predawn to well past midnight. Busy as he was, he nonetheless had noticed that he was popping an awfully a lot of antacid tablets lately. He'd had heartburn and indigestion for some time, but now it was getting really bad. He was feeling stressed. There were just too many things going on in his life. New demands on the job. Dissatisfied constituents. Political enemies taking potshots at him. Now, his five-year-old son was in the hospital. The doctors weren't sure what was wrong. Mike couldn't make it to the hospital during the day, so he was there with the boy late into the night, often sleeping overnight in the chair by his bedside. When the plumbing broke in his home that same week, he uncharacteristically started shouting. "Don't tell me I've got to deal with this, too!" he railed. Later that evening, he talked with his wife. His conclusion: "I'm just not myself lately. But I can handle it. We'll get through this."

That's how Mike ended up in the hospital with a bleeding ulcer. He saw the signs but didn't heed their message until his resistance to the changes taking place in his life sent him to the hospital. While laying in his sickbed, he had ample time to re-evaluate his life situation. He realized his increasing stress was the result of several factors: first, the political climate had changed dramatically since he was first elected seven years ago and he was losing his passion for politics; second, he was a father now. Family was important to him, but between campaigning and fund-raising and carrying out his role as a commissioner, he had little time for any personal life. He and his wife wanted to have another child. And now, his son was ill and there was no cure at hand.

The heartburn, the stomachaches, the packets of antacids, the sense of feeling overwhelmed, the long hours, the late nights, the sick boy, the changing political realities—all were signals. As much as Mike wanted to say they didn't matter and he could take it, they did matter. Mike's problems were eating him up. He had to face the fact that he was no longer happy with his life and it was no longer working. His heart was going in one direction; his career in another. It was time for a change.

Like Mike, we must accept that what's happening, or how we're changing, *does* matter. We need to grasp the significance of the signs we're noticing and take them seriously.

Are there signs you're dismissing? Are you toughing it out? Are you pretending things are okay, when actually they're not? Is there something eating at you? What new information or situations in your life do you need to take into account? Take the time to understand what they mean for you and your future. Is it time for a change?

BELIEVE THE SIGNS: BE PROACTIVE

For the past ten years, we've had the occasion to interview leaders repeatedly in over a hundred different fields. Over this period of time, most of these industries have undergone the most dramatic transformations in their histories. Some fields, like typesetting and typing services, have virtually disappeared. Others, like executive search and newsletter publication, are so different in nature as to require entirely different skills to do well. One thing has remained the same, however. Established industry leaders can be the least likely to grasp the scope and scale of the changes going on around them. Too often they're like the horse trader who asserted horseless carriages would never put him out of business because they scare the horses. Today's leaders often just don't believe they have much to worry about.

That's precisely what happened to Clarissa. If you recall, her referral business was dwindling, but she attributed it to an extended seasonal downturn. The point came when she did acknowledge that people could get services like hers for free on the Internet, but for the longest time, she was convinced that if she just cut back on her expenses, she would be okay. "There will always be people who want a live human being to talk to," she told herself. As the days passed before she had to close her business, she vacillated between feeling out of control and becoming overly perfectionistic for fear that if she made even one slipup, she would go under.

What Clarissa needed is what we all need in times of change: clarity about what's really happening and what aspects of it we can and can't control. If she had been clear as to what was happening, like Annette did in realizing that first the fax machine and then the Internet would change the nature of her business, Clarissa might have been able to sell her referral service for a handsome figure to a start-up dot.com company. Or, she might have morphed it into a web marketing company, helping her regular subscribers to establish their web presence. In other words, clarity about what was going on would have enabled her to be proactive and could have prevented her from concluding, as she did after her business went under, that her fate was out of her control.

Limiting or shortsighted beliefs about what is happening can also prevent us from making changes we want to initiate ourselves. If you recall, Donald had misgivings about his work as a marketing executive for some time, but he didn't believe that there were any other options unless he gave up the lifestyle he wanted to preserve. After his wake-up call of being unable to continue an important presentation, however, he knew he had to change and soon left the company he'd been working for. Eventually, he saw that he did have options. He started his own marketing company representing socially conscious companies, and, ultimately, his annual earnings exceeded that of his previous salary!

Gaining clarity means distinguishing what we hope will happen, fear could happen, and are programmed to think will happen from what actually *is* happening. It's the ability to observe objectively what needs to be done.

What beliefs are preventing you from looking at your current situation objectively? What trends are you hearing or reading about that you'd just as soon not believe? What changes do these developments suggest you consider making? What beliefs are causing you to conclude you can't do what you know you want and need to do? How could you see your way to concluding differently? How have others made the kind of changes you want to make?

Do You Get It?

Trying to ignore or resist a change that's happening is quite uncomfortable. It's like trying to get by in a suit of clothes you've outgrown or wearing a pair of shoes that pinch your feet. You can't do it for long without splitting your pants or getting blisters. But sometimes, we just don't get it. We keep limping along with our shirttail hanging out. How about you? Do you get it? Are you ready to acknowledge that it's time to move on? Test your readiness:

- Are you facing what's going on in your life, or are you pretending everything's fine? If you're not making the changes you need to be making, it's not fine, and, as you'll discover, it will only get worse.
- Do you have a nagging concern you keep pushing aside? Take it seriously. Stop ignoring it or putting up with it. Admit something's not right. You can't change it until you acknowledge it.
- Are others nagging you to acknowledge situations in your family, career, and personal life? Start listening to them. They could be trying to tell you something you need to hear.
- Is the world sending you a message you're not hearing? When change is under way, you'll keep getting a barrage of messages telling you that you need to take action until you do.
- Are you feeling eaten up by your problems? Chronic aches and pains can be your body's way of trying to cope with the stress of resisting changes you need to make.
- Do you feel limited, stifled, or smothered in your current situation? It's time to look at your beliefs. What's keeping you from moving on? It's your job to get over, around, or under it.
- Are you chronically unhappy with your situation? Chronic unhappiness is a signal that you've got to change. Even if you don't see how you can, accept that you must.

- Are you continuing to endure an ongoing painful or unpleasant situation? If so, it's like having a rock in our shoe way too long. If you don't want to have your foot amputated, you had better take it out.

- Are you feeling pressured? Pressure is a result of refusing to move. Sometimes, of course, you must take a stand and not bend to pressure. But is this one of those times, or is the pressure you're feeling an indication that you've gotten yourself in a pressure cooker and you need to take the lid off?

- Do you find yourself sighing or crying a lot? We do this when the circumstances of our lives are overwhelming, and we have to change them before things get better.

- Are there subjects and situations you simply won't talk about? Don't put up and shut up with what's bothering you. Get it out in the open in a trusted environment so you can do something about it.

- Are you waiting, expecting, or hoping for someone else to tell you how to take care of, coordinate, and manage the change you're facing? Changing directions is like giving birth to a child. Once you've conceived a child, no one but you can give birth to it. You can turn to others for support, guidance, suggestions, and ideas, but, ultimately, only you can make the final evaluation of your situation.

Hung Up? Getting Out of Stage One

"I'm needing to make some big changes," Harry told the group. "I'm in the process of re-evaluating my priorities." His friends had heard it before. In fact, it had become a joke among them. "Harry's re-evaluating his priorities again," they'd say with mock surprise, a wink, and a chuckle. It had been his mantra for the past five years, ever since his job as a manager for a Fortune 1000 company had been cut in a corporate buyout. Since then, Harry had been stuck in a rut. He'd been bouncing from one "temporary" position to another "just until I decide what I want to do next in my life."

While Harry obfuscated, his wife was becoming increasingly frustrated. Lately, she'd really been putting on the pressure. They were getting by financially, but they had five children, the first of whom was about to go to high school. Ten nonstop years of college tuition were only four years away. Harry knew he needed to make some big changes, and he'd had plenty of time to make them. But with the growing pressure from his wife, he was in a sweat about why he was still just talking instead of doing what needed to be done.

Perhaps you can relate to Harry's situation. Since you're reading this book, you undoubtedly know you need to make some changes in the direction your life is taking. But, like Harry, you may not be able to get past the stage of talking or thinking about the changes you need to make. There are a variety of "hang-ups" that can prevent us from moving on. Here are the most common:

BLOCKED: SUFFERING FROM A CHRONIC EMOTIONAL HEAD COLD

As we mentioned, change stirs up everything. If you accept that you have to change now, not later, not someday, but *now*, feelings of self-doubt, blame, worthlessness, and fears that you won't be able to have what you want, and might even lose what you have, may come bubbling to the surface. As long as you can approach the idea of changing your life as an intellectual exercise of "what if's," you won't have to face all the unpleasant feelings of making a decision to change.

In Harry's case, he had been afraid to admit that he'd screwed up his career. Right before he was downsized, he had mouthed-off to his boss about a situation he felt needed to be confronted. He was a strong-willed person. He prided himself on always speaking his mind. Look what that had gotten him. In these "temp" situations, he didn't have to risk that again. He was free to lay things on the table, because he wasn't going to be there very long, anyway.

But the pressure from putting his life on hold was forcing him to look at his feelings about his situation. This not only brought up his fears but also his guilt for having jeopardized his family's security and his shame for not living up to his own career expectations. He felt embarrassed to be around his friends, who were still steadily climbing their own career ladders despite their own setbacks and challenges. By continually "re-evaluating," he hoped they would excuse his lack of progress and think of him as a thoughtful and sincere professional.

Denying and burying all these feelings was like having a bad chronic head cold that won't break until your nose starts running. Harry's decision-making process was congested. He needed to allow himself to experience these painful feelings so he could understand his situation and move on. Acknowledging his feelings freed him to stop re-evaluating and start deciding. He had a few dark days at first, as the weight of his feelings about how his life had changed sank in. But soon, he could feel his energy moving forward again. Ideas began flowing as he confronted his fears, guilt, shame, and disappointment. Once brought into his conscious awareness, many of his fears and his judgments of himself were unjustified and irrational. He could make peace with them and move on.

What feelings are you holding back by not moving on in your life? What do you need to face before you can move on? Looking at what's bothering you opens the door to new possibilities.

DISBELIEF: HOPING IT'S NOT SO

"This can't be happening to me," Carla kept telling herself. "It just can't be." We've already mentioned how difficult it is to accept changes that we don't want to make. But refusing to admit we're changing, and hanging on to hope that we won't have to, is probably the most common way people get hung up at this stage. We saw the effect it had on Clarissa and her referral business. Her refusal to accept the change in her market complicated her life, but she had to accept it before long, like it or not. Her business was drying up, and her dwindling bank balance pushed her into Stage Two—saying goodbye to her business. For Carla, the situation was different.

Carla had trained for many years to become a psychologist. After completing years of formal education, she put in a grueling schedule to accumulate the required number of treatment hours for little or no pay so she could qualify to take her licensing exam. She endured the rigors of passing extensive written and oral exams. She had done all this while working full-time in a job she couldn't wait to leave. At last, she was a psychologist! She took a job at a respected hospital but quickly discovered she didn't like working in a hospital setting. She left that position for one in a private counseling center. But all too soon, she found it was also unfulfilling.

She was impatient with her clients. Delighted when they canceled. Eager to leave as early as possible. Hated the staff conferences. At first, she blamed her supervisor's insistence on formal record-taking. Then she decided it was this agency's policies that bothered her. So she took a more independent position where she would have full responsibility for selecting and working with her own clients in her own way. Still, she couldn't wait for the last client to leave at the end of the day.

Since she was actually a competent professional, she could have gone on forever in this fashion. And for quite a while she did. Whenever the possibility occurred to her that she really didn't like working as a psychologist, she simply dismissed it, and there was no one or nothing to force her to do otherwise. One day, however, she was about to tell her client it was time for her to refer him to another professional when she realized she wanted to tell that to all her clients! "This can't be. This can't be," she cried over and over again, when later that night she couldn't get to sleep. But it was. She was not happy with her chosen career.

She loved studying psychology. She liked being a psychologist. She liked completing her training program. But she didn't like "doing" psychotherapy. Her fantasy of what it would be like and the reality of doing it were quite different. While she kept hoping this would change, it didn't, but it wasn't until she stopped hoping it would change that she could start thinking about what she actually liked about her field. At heart, she concluded, she was an academic. She wanted to teach and write about her chosen profession, not engage in the clinical practice of it.

Is there something you're hoping isn't true? Only when you give up false hopes will you find what you're really hoping for.

FEAR OF THE UNKNOWN:
FROZEN IN THE HEADLIGHTS

No doubt about it. Fear shuts us down. Like a deer in the headlights, it paralyzes us, leaving us frozen in the very place we don't want to be. We don't see options. The energy drains from our bodies and we can't mobilize our resources. Immobilized by fear, we become indecisive, uncertain of the right decisions to make.

So, securing your immediate well-being is key to being able to change directions. To change directions, you must be grounded in a place from which to move. If you're feeling like a deer in the headlights, your first priority must be to create as safe a situation for yourself as possible. For Susan, this meant lining up a secure job as soon as she was released from the alcohol rehab treatment center. No matter that it wasn't the best-paying job or the most interesting one. She simply had to get on her feet again. It was a matter of survival. For Denise, who could no longer work as a forest ranger, it meant moving home with her parents again so she could be cared for while she recovered from her illness and decided upon a new career direction. For Clarrisa, who had to close her referral business after not heeding the signs of a changing market, it meant taking a salaried position at the company where she used to work until she could decide if she wanted to start another business and, if so, doing what.

Getting out of the headlights means finding out everything you can about how others have handled situations similar to the changes you're dealing with. It means bringing out your real concerns and attending to what needs to be attended to in order to put them to rest. To get moving, stop worrying, and start wondering. If you have difficulty relaxing enough, put your creativity to work to get away from the intensity and high stimulation that your changing situation is creating. Clear your mind so you get clear about what you need to do next.

It's also vital to do your homework and begin creating a series of small successes you can build upon. When Vicki left her editorial position, for example, her colleagues and friends were scared for her. "How will you make it? How will you ever earn enough money on your own? You know how many starving writers there are!" But Vicki had secured her future. Before leaving her job, she arranged to do some freelance work on a three-year contract with the newspaper where she'd been working. Even though she'd written many articles about business start-ups and interviewed a slew of successful business owners as a reporter, to ensure that she was starting out on a solid foundation, she enrolled in a college course on starting a business. She also came to our *Get Away for a Change* workshop.

SHOCK: SHATTERED BY TRAUMA

Pete and Edie had just lost their twenty-one-year-old daughter to AIDS. Her decline had been swift but excruciatingly painful and debilitating, over what seemed like an endless few months. She had moved back home with Pete and Edie who had cared for her in shifts, day and night, over this time. Meanwhile, Pete's union had gone out on strike over contract negotiations. Edie's part-time teaching job was suddenly their only source of income. Their savings went down fast, spent on medications and rental costs of home health care equipment. When this ordeal was finally over, their home was in foreclosure, they had filed for bankruptcy, and the union was still on strike. But Pete and Edie pooled their remaining resources and headed off for a month of travel in France.

Friends and neighbors were shocked and disapproving. How could they take a costly trip under such circumstances? How irresponsible! But the couple returned from their sojourn renewed and energized. They came home to greet their son and daughter-in-law and met their first grandchild. They rented a small apartment in a new neighborhood near Edie's son. Pete went back to work under a new and improved union contract, while Edie began a new career writing a book about caring for a dying child. Their life was not back to "usual." It never would be. But they were moving ahead in new directions.

Hopefully, most of us will never have to suffer through a trauma like this, but many changes, especially undesirable ones, are traumatic. When all the rules have changed or the rug has been pulled out from under you, it's difficult to jump back up and leap enthusiastically into new possibilities. If you've been laid off, suffered a life-altering injury or disease, been through a difficult divorce, were forced to close your business, failed at a lifelong dream, or any other equally disturbing or disappointing life circumstance, you have sustained a shock to your system. Your identity may be frayed or fragile. Your confidence in yourself and your trust in life may be shaken.

By taking a month-long trip to Paris, Pete and Edie had taken the time they needed to recover from the trauma of the changes they'd been undergoing. By getting away from the life they'd known before their daughter's death, they were able to accept the reality of the changes that had taken place and were ready to move on when they returned. If you have been traumatized by change, you, too, may need to take time off and get away so you won't get mired in reminders of your miseries. While Paris might not be the practical or preferred choice for you, if you're feeling traumatized by the changes you're going through, think of what you need to do to recover, regenerate, and recharge yourself so you can move on.

TURBO FUEL: To Recover Your Equilibrium, Create a Personal Sanctuary

If you can't go to your favorite getaway, create one of your own right where you are. Find a quiet, comfortable place where you won't be interrupted. Sit back and close your eyes and imagine a place where you feel completely relaxed, energized, and inspired. You can extend the benefits of such mini-mental vacations by creating an area in your home where you can retreat. It can be a corner of your bedroom, an attic alcove, a bathroom hideaway, or an entire bedroom, just for you. Decorate this area with your favorite colors and favorite things. Be sure you have a comfortable chair or couch where you can totally relax and meditate. Even ten minutes a day in your personal sanctuary can be immensely helpful. Add whatever touches will help you feel at peace. Your favorite music. A cup of hot tea. Meaningful photographs. A book of poetry or prayers. Whatever you treasure.

In today's hectic lifestyle, creating and getting away to your own personal sanctuary may mean finding someone to watch the kids, taking a personal day off work, or booting your cousin from New Jersey out of the guest room. Whatever it takes, if you need the space to recover from recent traumas, you've got to make a place where you can do it.

TOO OVERWHELMED AND HELPLESS: REDUCED TO A BLOB OF JELLO

Whether the changes in your life are about getting out of a undesirable situation you're in or adapting to a painful one you've been presented with, most of us don't put up with an unpleasant situation for long unless we think nothing can be done about it. Sometimes, like Mike, the county commissioner with the ill five-year-old, our circumstances simply seem too overwhelming to do anything about except to just dig in and plunge ahead. When Mike told his wife, "I can handle this. We'll get through it," what he really meant was "There's nothing I can do about this, anyway."

When we allow ourselves to be overwhelmed by the enormity or impossibility of whatever change we're facing, we feel helpless. If you're in this situation, if you hear yourself saying, "Well there's nothing I can do about this," you need to do two things: first, break whatever you're dealing with into a series of small segments you can address, one by one; second, start asking yourself, "What can I do about this?" Mike, for example, couldn't solve his son's medical problem on his own. He wasn't a doctor. Nor could he neglect his responsibilities as a commissioner in order to spend all his time at the hospital. He also couldn't quell all his dissatisfied constituents and political enemies overnight. But he didn't have to put up with his situation. Once Mike started talking with his wife about the situation and how he felt, he began to realize there were things he could do, and those things would set in motion the changes that would eventually improve his life.

For example, recognizing that he was losing his passion for politics opened up the possibility of not running for office in the next year's election. This would immediately free him from the endless round of fund-raising dinners and late-night activities that were keeping him from getting to the hospital until after midnight. It would also eliminate most of the attacks by his enemies. He'd be gone in a year, anyway, so they would move on to skirmish with others who were still in the game. So that's exactly what Mike decided to do, and the minute he made the decision not to run for office, his life got back on keel. His problems, while still difficult, had shrunk to a manageable size. This one decision that was within Mike's control put him back in charge. He was no longer helpless or overwhelmed.

Mike reclaimed his equilibrium and moved on with his life by talking things through with his wife and understanding the reality of his situation.

Are you telling yourself there's nothing you can do about your situation? What if you decided there was something you could do about it, even if you don't know what it is yet? What if, instead of saying, "I can't do anything about this," you started asking yourself, "What can I do about this?" How could you break down what you're dealing with into one small thing you could do something about? Start talking with others you trust about how you're feeling and what you think.

Changing directions can be an emotional roller coaster. Fear, shocked, being overwhelmed, and helplessness will come up again in future chapters in relation to different aspects of change, along with a myriad of other emotions. All the emotions you may be experiencing right now, from excitement about the new directions your life is taking to anxiety about whether they will turn out well for you, can each be a helpful signal for what you need to do next. So pay attention to your emotions during this time. They will help you keep moving and prevent you from getting hung up or, at least, not for long. For more information on understanding and benefiting from the emotions you're having at this stage of changing your life, see the appendix: *A Guide to Handling the Emotions of Change.*

The best thing about facing the reality of change is that once you do, you're on your way. There's no turning back. The only way to go is forward. The time has come to say goodbye to what has been.

Is your future on hold? What are you waiting for? How could you begin working toward your future right now, even if its in some small way?

Breakthrough: Roland

It was only another five years to early retirement, but to Roland that seemed a lifetime. His heart had moved on, but his body still had to be on the job where he worked as a youth counselor. He could feel himself becoming more lethargic and discouraged with each passing week. Even his family was noticing his growing impatience.

We met Roland by chance through his wife, and he began telling us how much he wanted to move on. "I'm taking flying lessons now," he said with a glimmer of excitement streaking briefly across his eyes. "I know I'll never be able to earn a living from flying, but I enjoy it. What I want to do is earn the income I need from writing."

Writing, it turns out, had been a long-standing interest of Roland's, and he was more than ready to get into it, but he was waiting for retirement. We could see that keeping his dreams on hold was sapping the life out of him, so we suggested he need not wait. He could start preparing now, building a writing practice on the side. The idea energized him immediately. He began looking through our book, *Best Home Businesses for the 21st Century,* and decided upon technical writing. Suddenly, his enthusiasm for life returned. He was no longer stuck.

He began building his technical writing business on the side, which he continues to do at this time. Now that he's no longer waiting, even his attitude and energy for his regular job have also changed. It's no longer something to endure but a springboard to a new future.

CLOSING REFLECTION

Think of yourself as standing on a hillside looking down upon your life as it has been up to this point. What have you been doing? Who have you been? When did it appear that it was time for a change? How did you know? How do you feel about the need to change?

Facing reality screws you up less than denying it.
—RICHARD NORTH PATTERSON, *DARK LADY*

SAYING **G**OODBYE **T**O **W**HERE **Y**OU'VE **B**EEN:

RELEASING THE PAST

Opportunity is often disguised as a loss.

—MEGAN EDWARDS

We had been hired to speak to a group of outplaced executives about new career alternatives. We would be focusing on exploring possibilities for them to start their own businesses. It was a gathering of over twenty people, and the group leader suggested that the participants introduce themselves to us. They began to do so by going around the room one by one:

"Hi, I'm . . . I was a manager of . . . for the . . . Corporation . . . "

"I'm . . . For the past ten years I was working as . . . "

"Hello, I was an account executive for . . . "

And so the introductions went as we moved around the room. "I was . . ." "I was . . ." "I was . . ." "I have been . . ." "I have been . . ." Each person was defining himself or herself by the role he or she had been in before being terminated. Every so often, someone would say "I am . . ." They were using the present tense "I am" to describe the role we thought they'd had been down-sized from.

We were confused. Were some of these people still employed? Were some of them in the outplacement program to decide whether to leave their current positions? No, we ascertained. Each executive in this group knew he or she was out of his job. None would be going back. They either had to get new jobs or somehow change careers. They'd been out of work for several weeks to several months. To one degree or another, however, they were all still defining themselves in terms of their past positions with a particular company. They knew they were facing a new reality, but it was clear to us that they had not said goodbye to their past.

Neither had Jeanette. Six weeks after she completed the last of a twenty-six-week series as the talk-show host on a new cable television show, Jeanette heard some great news. The show was being renewed for another twenty-six weeks. Jeanette was elated when a co-worker called with the news. She dialed up the producer at once to congratulate him. She was thinking about throwing a party for the whole cast and crew. They'd worked so hard for such long hours. They'd been through so much together, but now it was all paying off!

This moment was especially elevating for Jeanette. She had dreamed of having her own talk show for many years. Fifteen years of acting lessons; stand-up-comic, open-mike nights; negotiating with agents; reading for talent coordinators; going for callbacks, screen tests, and demos shoots; glad-handing at cable trade shows and taping pilots, all the while holding down a high-pressure telemarketing job she hated in order to finance her lifelong ambition. During all those years, though, she had never given up hope. Now, finally, her dream had come true, and, despite all the pressure, the long hours, and the hard work, she loved every minute of it. She loved the show. She loved her role. The producer and crew loved her and she loved them. They were like family.

When the producer didn't take her call, Jeanette thought nothing of it. He was always incredibly busy. She left a voice-mail message and expected a call back any time. The hours passed into days, and by the following Monday afternoon, when she realized he'd never called back, a bolt of fear ripped through her chest, "What if . . . ?" She called again and left another voice-mail message, trying to sound as upbeat and cheery as possible. Still no word. Her anxiety grew. She called her agent and several others from the cast and crew. No one was picking up. She hardly slept that night. "This couldn't be happening," she kept telling herself. But it was. The next morning, there was a FedEx from her agent.

He wanted her to know that the producer appreciated her contribution to the show immensely and enjoyed working with her. The network was taking the show in a new direction, however, and they needed a new "look." "Not to worry, though," the agent added. "We'll find something else for you. I'll call soon."

That was six months ago. Although Jeanette realized she wouldn't be resuming her role on that show, she was so devastated, she couldn't muster the energy to call her agent about other possibilities, and, of course, he hadn't called her. Episodes of the new show began airing, and the new host was at least ten years younger than Jeanette, probably not even twenty years old. The message was clear: they wanted a younger host to attract the younger audience the network desired. "It's not right, it's not fair," she lamented. Still, she blamed herself. She just wasn't young enough or pretty enough. With a probable life expectancy of ninety-plus, at thirty-six she was past her prime.

Jeanette tried going back to her telemarketing job, but she felt too anxious and exhausted to work. She suffered dizzy spells and couldn't concentrate, but the little savings she'd set aside from the show were dwindling. She knew she had to make a change. She either had to give up her dream or jump back in and pursue it again with vigor. But her heart was still longing for the limelight of six months ago. She couldn't say goodbye to a dream that had died.

Neither could Marjorie, but for her it had been over a year. In her mid-fifties, Marjorie was recovering from a divorce, and everyone thought she was doing quite well. After thirty years of marriage, her husband, a neurosurgeon, had announced he was leaving her for another woman. The settlement was ample. She still lived in the same large home in a lovely tree-lined neighborhood. Uncomfortable with continuing her volunteer work for the hospital where her ex-husband worked, however, Marjorie had started her own home-based business as an interior decorator. But her daughter thought it was time for Marjorie to get some help with her business because it wasn't progressing. That's how we met her.

When she came for her appointment, she talked of everything except her business. The divorce. The lawsuits she'd filed against her ex-husband that were still pending. Her grandbabies and how she couldn't bear to go to family parties to see them if her husband and his new trophy wife were present. What he had said the last time she ran into him at one of these parties. How much she missed being president of the hospital's volunteer organization, etc., etc. She didn't really have enough time to devote to her business, she explained, although she was sure it would be a success once she was able to "clear her plate" of all these other responsibilities.

Right or wrong, fair or unjust, for better or worse, it's hard to move forward when you're looking backward.

Are you trying to walk backward into the future? Are you holding on to aspects of the past and preventing yourself from moving on?

The Task: Pulling Your Energy Out of What Has Been

Change is always accompanied by loss. It is a birth, death, and renewal process. In change, you leave behind aspects of who you are. You leave behind elements of what you do. You leave behind some of what you've had. Even when you're looking forward to the changes you're making, there are certain things you must give up in order to move on. Of course, there is much to gain from a new direction as well, even if you're not all that excited about having to change. But often, whether or not a change is wanted, there will be a lag between what must die and the birth of what will come.

Like the ruins of an ancient building, aspects of what has been in our lives must collapse before we can build a new life upon their remains. Obviously, the less a change requires us to let go of, the easier this transition will be. But we each have a level of change we can tolerate comfortably, and how we respond to change is based on our personal experiences and how we've seen our family and friends deal with change.

According to psychologist Morris Massey, we form our basic beliefs and frame of reference about life, including how we view change, between the ages of eight and twelve. Of course, in past generations, change usually occurred more gradually, but many of our parents and grandparents lived through the Great Depression, World War II, Vietnam, the Gulf War, or other difficult times. All these traumas changed their lives forever and affected how they felt about change from that time forward. We grew up watching them live out those decisions throughout our childhood. Their habits, thoughts, and actions helped to form ours.

What was going on in your parents' lives when they were eight to twelve years old? How did those or other events shape your family's Change History? How did that history affect you? What was going on in your life when you were eight to twelve years old? How has that shaped your own personal history with change? How has your upbringing or personal experiences shaped the way you feel about change? Has change been primarily a positive experience for you, or has it been a difficult and stressful one? How have you responded to other changes in your life?

Bonnie had just told the group what she wanted to do to change directions. There was a long silence; everyone was aware of the same incongruity. There was absolutely no joy in her voice or on her face as she talked about her plans. Carefully, the group members began to explore their concerns. "Are you sure this is what you really want to do?" "Is this what you'd do if you could do anything?"

At first, Bonnie was resolute, "Yes, this is what I want." But as the group remained puzzled, Bonnie could feel how much they wanted to enthusiastically support her choice. After another moment of silence, she looked slowly around the room at the faces of those present and began to explain. "To understand my decision, you've got to understand my family background," she volunteered. "My father was always a dreamer with wonderful, wild ideas. My mother was the practical one, the one who kept everything together. In pursuing one of his grand ideas, my father got with the wrong people and ended up in prison. But he served his term and settled down after that. He had the same job with an electronic store the rest of his life. And we were all much happier."

Bonnie paused, then went on. " I've always been like my father at heart. I have all these wild ideas. But it's a dangerous trait, and so, all my life I've tried to be more like my mother. As you can see, it's better that way."

We all could see how it had worked out well for Bonnie to be like her mother. She had a steady job, a good income, a lovely condo of her own, a nice car. But now she wanted to change jobs, and her plans looked like a carbon copy of what she was saying she wanted to leave behind.

As Bonnie reflected on her family's change history and wrote in her change journal about how it was affecting her decisions, she realized her father's history was limiting her future. She decided it was time to explore the value of some of her "wild ideas," which turned out to be more exotic than wild.

Bonnie decided to enroll in a college program to become a marine mammal trainer. At first, her mother couldn't imagine what had come over Bonnie, but after she graduated she landed a great job at a marine world facility, and even her mother could see what a great choice her new direction was. "I've always loved animals," she had told the group so many months before, and now she was earning a living working with them.

Whether it stems from our upbringing, personal experience, or genetic makeup, some people enjoy lots of radical change. They can cast off one life for another like a change of clothing. Others would prefer things to stay pretty much the same over their lifetime. Changing their lives is no more appealing than having a root canal, and it's just as painful. Most of us, however, like a little change here and there, as long as it's for the better and things won't be all that different.

How about you? To find out your change comfort level, ask yourself this question: What is the relationship between your line of work this year and your line of work last year? Write your answer in your change journal. Then read through what you've written and notice whether you have described the relationship as:

____ *the same, similar, no different*
____ *different, changed, new*
____ *somewhat the same or different, with exceptions expressed by using words like "mostly," "like better," "more or less," "evolving," "improving," "except for," "although," etc.*

According to behavioral researcher Rodger Bailey, most people, about 65 percent, like things to change gradually for the better. About 25 percent of us seek frequent, dramatic changes, and a few, around 5 percent, want things to remain as they have been, now and forever. Your comfort level with change, and the degree of change you're being called upon to make, will determine how easily you can pull your energy out of the direction you've been headed and start moving in a new direction.

What have you lost or what will you be losing as a result of the changes that are taking place in your life? What will be no more? Make a list in your journal of everything you already miss, or fear you will miss, as the current changes in your life unfold.

Regardless of our comfort level with change, if we are to move on, one way or another, we must let go of who we have been and redirect how we're investing our time, our money, and our energy. Here are several of the tasks we must complete to move through this stage.

Look in the Mirror: It's Time for a Makeover

We once worked with a hairstylist who specializes in makeovers. Watching him at work, we saw people undergo dramatic transformations right before our eyes. His clients would leave the styling chair looking great. Most of them, both men and women, reported feeling marvelous about themselves once they saw their new image in the mirror. "Wow," we commented, "you must find this work so rewarding!" Well, he told us, he would be candid. While he does enjoy his work, in reality, about 80 percent of the people who come to him for makeovers, regardless of how great they feel about their new look, revert right back to their old look once they return to their regular routines. The reason they give: "I looked great, but it wasn't really me."

Just like these folk, Jeanette, Marjorie, and the executives in the outplacement program we described earlier were all having trouble with getting a makeover, but that's what their lives were demanding. Until they were able to see themselves in a new light, they were not going to change. The professionals in the outplacement program had an image of themselves as executives who went to work everyday in suits and ties so they could carry out a particular role within their companies. That role had become who they were. Without it, they no longer knew who they were, so they were desperately clinging to who they had been. Jeanette couldn't let go of the image of herself as the talk-show host with her own cable show. It was who she'd always wanted to be and who she had at last become. Marjorie was the doctor's wife, the president of the hospital auxiliary, the mother, and now a grandmother. That's the person she'd been for thirty years. She liked that person and didn't want to be anyone else.

The words, the deeds, the demeanor, everything about these individuals was out of step with the person their changing lives were expecting them to become. Before they could move on, they would have to say goodbye to the person they had been, turn around and walk away to discover who they could be. The outplaced executives needed to stop introducing themselves as who they had been and start introducing themselves as who they wanted to be. They needed to stop carrying around their old business cards and have new ones made that describe who they are now.

The outplaced execs are no longer managers for XYZ Corporation, just as Marjorie is no longer the doctor's wife and Jeanette is no longer the talk-show host, nor is she the telemarketer she was before that. Each of these individuals needed to look in the mirror and see someone different. Before we can become someone new, we have to give up thinking of ourselves as who we were and start accepting ourselves as who we are now.

Who have you been? Who are you now? Who do you want to be? Do you know yet? You may not. Often, it takes time to accept that we are no longer who we were and only then can we begin to imagine who we will become.

This redefinition of our identity isn't a challenge just for those of us who are coping with unwanted change. It also affects those of us who are making a desired change. Keith, for example, had lived in the same Midwestern town all his life. But his dream since childhood had been to move some day to New York. He had climbed the corporate ladder to regional sales manager for a small pharmaceutical company when suddenly his lifelong dream became a possibility. There was an opening for a similar position with the same company in New York.

Keith quickly applied for and landed the job. Everyone in his family and the company was happy for him. He was happy, too, at first. But as moving day approached, he grew increasingly morose, although he put on a happy face while making the rounds of farewell parties and throughout the move. After all, his wife and two daughters were having their own adjustments to make so that Keith could pursue his dream, so regardless of his unexpected sad feelings, he was determined to move ahead. Soon, he and his family were living not in a sprawling green suburb but in an attached urban brownstone. Keith had outfitted himself with a new wardrobe more in keeping with his Eastern clientele and, before long, started wearing contact lenses instead of glasses and sporting a trendier hairstyle.

Still, his gloomy mood wasn't lifting. He was easily irritated and, despite loving his new job and being in the heart of all the action of New York City, he was constantly complaining about this or that inconvenience . . . until he finally admitted he was homesick. He missed his parents. The church. The old neighborhood. Having beer with the guys after work at the pub. Playing basketball with his old high school buddies down at the park where they'd played since grade school. In New York, he was becoming someone else—an Easterner. After realizing how he felt, Keith took off a few days and flew home. There, he could revisit and grieve for the person he'd been, say goodbye to the life he'd known, and return to his new home as the new person he was becoming.

Mourn: It's the Only Way
to Really Say Goodbye

Unlike Keith, when Connie and Chris decided to take a job in California co-directing a special education program, they knew right away that saying goodbye to their friends and family wasn't going to be easy. They had spent their past five vacations in northern California. One summer they looked at each other and asked, "Why don't we live here? Other people do. Why not us? This is where we want to be." Hence, they began planning how they would alter their careers to move to northern California and start a new life.

Not feeling that they could restart their small business in a totally new community, they started looking on the Internet for jobs they could do together, and sooner than they had imagined, they found a co-director position with a small nonprofit organization. Although pleased with the prospect of their new future, they both found themselves crying throughout the days that followed, as they did one thing after another for the last time. They got teary-eyed while shopping in their favorite stores and eating at their favorite restaurants. They choked up while feeding the big elm tree in their backyard for the last time. They misted up while packing up their office furniture for the closeout sale.

Connie and Chris were sobered by the fact that they were no longer going to be their own boss. In California, they would have jobs again, a board supervising their performance, regular hours, and a paycheck. They decided to make a collage with reminders of their business, and, before closing the doors, they launched the final close outsale with a big party for all their regular customers and suppliers. There were many teary-eyed, fond farewells, but those were nothing compared to the tearful goodbyes with friends and, finally, with family. They spent the last night before moving day with Connie's parents, who were happy to see them pursue their dreams but heartbroken about losing their family to a two thousand-mile airplane trip.

The morning of the move, both their families came over for a farewell pancake breakfast and helped the couple pack the kids, the two dogs, and random luggage into their SUV (sports utility vehicle). As Chris and Connie drove away, they looked back into the sunrise to wave goodbye one last time, and then they turned west and never looked back again. They had grieved for what they were leaving behind and were ready to greet what lay ahead.

Sadness and sorrow are healthy responses to a loss of any kind, forced or chosen. It helps to emotionally let go of what can no longer be. Grief purges our feelings of loss and prevents us from getting stuck in them. We've noticed, for example, that neither by design nor invitation, there are always lots of spontaneous tears during the first morning of our changing-directions workshops. By lunchtime, however, participants are feeling joyous and free to move on, because the tears of saying goodbye are cleansing tears. They are tears of release and letting go.

Have you allowed yourself to cry and grieve for what you're leaving behind? Or are you holding in your feeling of loss, pretending you don't care or maintaining a stiff upper lip? Review the list of what you've lost or will be losing and allow yourself to feel whatever feelings you have about saying goodbye to these aspects of your life. What events or activities would help you to say goodbye? Who do you need to talk with? What do you need to share?

TURBO FUEL: Healthy Comfort Food

In the midst of change, we often get hungry for our favorite comfort foods. But too often, the foods we crave at such times are actually not ones that are good for us. Cookies, candy, chips, soft drinks, coffee, alcohol, and junk food in general don't actually nourish, fortify, or cleanse our bodies. Instead, they tend to blow us out, hype us up, or dull our senses just when we need to be energized, calm, relaxed, and alert. The unhealthy comfort foods we crave account for why many of us gain weight during major life changes.

There are, however, comfort foods that will nourish, satisfy, and fulfill us. Such foods are generally alkaline in nature, like fruits and vegetables, balanced in protein, fat, and carbohydrates, and suited to our own physiology. The following is a recipe for one our favorite Healthy Comfort snacks. Try it:

Healthy Comfort Food Recipe

Slice Medjool dates in half, remove pits.

*Nestle a small amount of your favorite low- or nonfat cheese in the hollow
of each half date.*

Place one half walnut on top of cheese.

Warm in microwave or toaster oven until cheese is soft.

Pop in mouth and enjoy!

Look for other healthy comfort foods in the upcoming chapters.

CLEAR THE CALENDAR: IT'S A NEW DAY

You may recall that Marjorie, the woman who was starting an interior decorating business after a difficult divorce, was eager to talk about nearly everything except her new business. No wonder she was having trouble getting it under way. She had not cleared her calendar for a new future. She was still filling her days reminiscing about the organization she once led, her grandkids, the lawsuits she was filing against her husband, etc. She was entirely too busy with concerns of the past to create a new life. As was Jeanette. She was spending hours preparing a scrapbook of her canceled cable show, talking on the phone with friends about their reaction to reruns of her shows, cataloging video copies of shows she'd kept as mementos, and so on.

Our lives tend to move in whatever direction we put our energy. We can easily get an objective picture of where we're actually headed, as opposed to where we say we're headed, by looking at how we spend our time, our money, and our energy. What we talk about, what we schedule into our day, what we spend our money on, are all mirrors for where our true energy lies. Both Jeanette and Marjorie put their energy into holding on to a life that could never be again. Thus, their lives were miserable, not because of the recent new hand life had dealt them but because of what they were choosing to do with that hand.

Of course, as with Roland who we featured in the last chapter in the **"Breakthroughs"** section, you may not be able to take your energy entirely away from your past or your current situation until you've built enough of a new future to stand on solidly. Roland plans to retire in four years, so he shows up for his job and does what he's required to do, but he's taken his "heart" energy out of his job. His heart energy is now going into building his new technical writing business and learning to fly.

When we run into Roland at the post office, for example, he never makes mention of his job. But he's eager to tell us about the progress he's made on his business and his most recent aerial exploits. He's altered his schedule to allow more time for both these activities, and he's putting his discretionary income into office equipment, software, and flying lessons. He's investing his energy in his future, not the past.

How do you spend your time? What do you talk about with friends, family, and colleagues? What are you saving your money for? What are you spending it on? The answers to these questions will tell you where your real interest lies right now and whether your future is more likely to look like the past, the present, or something entirely new.

Are You Ready to Let Go?

- Are you open to discovering that you are more than the person you've been in carrying out the roles and activities of your life up to this point?
- Are you ready to consider something new?
- Are you ready to give up what you hate in your life, even if it means others things will have to change?
- Are you ready to stop blaming yourself or others for whatever has happened that resulted in your needing to make changes in your life?
- Can you let go of whatever you've lost or will be losing so you can make room for what you could gain by making a change?
- Do you feel worthy of having a new life?
- Are you ready to stop pleasing others and start pleasing yourself?
- When it's possible to do so, can you turn and walk away from what has been and start putting your heart energy into something new?

Hung Up? Getting Out of Stage Two

Clearly, Marjorie and Jeanette were stuck in Stage Two. They couldn't say goodbye, so they couldn't move on. But, of course, their lives had changed, so by holding on, they were suffering. Jeanette wasn't feeling well enough to work. Marjorie was angry and bitter, consumed with making her husband pay for the misery he had caused her. Perhaps you can relate to their situations.

Perhaps you, too, want to hold on to the past. Perhaps you're still angry that your life has changed and feel that what's happened to you is unjust and unfair. You may still be looking back to better or easier times. It's understandable. Holding on to past hurts, anger, and injustice is the most common hang-up that prevents us from being able to say hello to a new life. Here are several ways to do that and how to let go.

DEPRESSION: RUN OVER BY A TWO-TON TRUCK

Depression is the most common result of holding on to a painful loss. It flattens us out like the coyote in one of those silly Roadrunner cartoons. It takes all the wind out of our sails and lets all the air out of our balloon. It turns off the glint in our eyes and puts out the fire in our bellies. We give up. We cave in. Or we desperately overdo and overwork until we're completely burned out and have nothing left to give. Either way, we end up physically and emotionally exhausted and fatigued. It's hard to concentrate. Even our eating and sleeping patterns can be affected. You can't and won't be able to go anywhere with your life as long as you're depressed.

If depression has become chronic and severe, professional or medical assistance is most likely essential, but if you're stuck in a mild depression, there are ways you can get out of it on your own. Depression is a signal that you aren't expressing the grief and pain and anger you feel. Instead, you're de-pressing, pressing down those feelings, numbing yourself to them and, in the process, to all other feelings as well. Thus, while you don't feel the pain of anger or disappointment when you're depressed, you also can no longer feel curious, excited, enthusiastic, loved, and interested. Yet these are the emotions that will enable you to tap into the new desires that could be growing in your heart, new desires that would enable you move on and create a new life.

The solution to depression is expression. You've got to start expressing your feelings. This will GET YOU MOVING. Jeanette, for example, after years of refusing to give up hope for her dream, felt hopeless and helpless in the face of the age discrimination she was experiencing in the television industry. She had driven and pushed herself mercilessly to overcome this barrier and briefly thought she'd won. She was exhausted from trying to make her dream happen and felt defeated by forces beyond her control.

Once Jeanette began to express her feelings, however, she realized she didn't have to allow the television industry to control her life. She considered filing an age discrimination lawsuit against the producer as a way to right the wrong she felt had been done to her. Instead, she decided that that would only further tether her to an industry where she was not appreciated. For years, she had been fighting an uphill battle in hostile territory. With the help of creative brainstorming, she began to see there were other arenas where her talents and abilities would be valued and appreciated. She began exploring possibilities, for example, of becoming a professional speaker or hosting an radio show on the Web.

Seeing new possibilities lifted her spirits and renewed her energy. She had new directions to explore and the confidence to take another job while she did so. But this time, she refused to take a job she hated. Instead, she took a position as an events coordinator, where one of her responsibilities was to emcee charity events.

TURBO FUEL: Dissolving Downers

When you're depressed, most of your energy is going into blocking the conscious awareness of your true feelings, leaving you depleted and weary. Once you acknowledge these feelings, however, you can direct all that freed-up energy back into your life. Here's one of our favorite ways to bypass the mental blocks that prevent us from knowing what we're really feeling. It's from diarist Tristine Rainer:

Sit with your change journal in a quiet, relaxed place. Close your eyes and let an image come to mind. Then write about this image and your reaction to it in your journal. Let its story unfold. How is it a tale of your life?

Example:

Image: I see an image of myself lying alone and abandoned in a dark, empty room. It looks like a prison. I have no food or water. It is cold and I am too weak to stand.

My reaction: My heart is breaking as I see myself lying there. I start crying for that woman who is me and rush to her side with blankets and water and a bowl of warm soup. She feels better immediately, although I continue crying with her for some time. Then we get up and leave the dark room together.

Meaning for my life: I need to start taking better care of myself right here and now. I close my journal and run a hot bath and continue to pamper myself all evening. It is more soothing to my soul than anything I can remember for a long time.

RESENTMENT: IMPRISONED BY OLD ANGER

While Jeanette was suffering from regret, Marjorie was stuck in anger. She was blaming herself for not being a younger, prettier, and sexier wife. She was blaming her husband for not loving her the way she was. But, most of all, she was blaming him for stealing her life from her. She had been raised to be "the doctor's wife." She had grown up in an upper middle-class family with a stay-at-home mom and believed a woman's duty was primarily at home and secondarily in doing community work.

For thirty years, her life had revolved around her family and the volunteer medical community. Now, although healthy and financially comfortable, she felt as if she had no life. Her children were grown, and activities with them usually brought her in contact in some way with her ex-husband. The vitriol of the divorce had soured her ability to participate in the hospital auxiliary with which her husband was affiliated. She was the odd-one-out with the couples at the country club, where she had socialized, golfed, and played tennis.

Marjorie found most people had little sympathy for her misery because, after all, few people were so well-off. So she kept most of her resentment to herself. Of course, it did, nonetheless, slip into casual comments to friends and resulted in all-too-frequent complaints to family members about her ex and his new wife. Mostly, though, she kept her resentment alive through a series of ongoing lawsuits against her ex-husband over various property and financial arrangements.

In truth, instead of getting even with her ex-husband through these lawsuits, Marjorie was turning over to him the power to control and direct her life. His leaving her had been painful. It had changed her life against her will. But now she was allowing her anger and resentment to prolong and continue her anguish. Once she began to realize this, she could see that she was the one being hurt most by her resentment. He was happily remarried. Her lawsuits and squabbles were nothing more than a few grains of sand in his shoe. "I started to see that the best way I could get even was to create a new life for myself." But to do that, to move on, Marjorie had to forgive him, not for his sake, but to free herself. She had to accept not what he had done, but that he had done it. In other words, she had to accept life as it was, if she were to make something new from it.

"I finally admitted that neither of us had been all that happy in our relationship for a long time," Marjorie confessed. "I liked my life. But I didn't really like him, and hadn't for many years. He had changed and I had changed."

Marjorie had met her husband in medical school, and after graduation, they married. She had given up the practice of medicine to become a wife and full-time mother. Now she was neither. Her decision to go into interior decorating had been a misguided effort to perpetuate her home-making role. "I didn't really want to decorate anyone else's home," she realized. "I was trying to re-create my role as the homemaker." But finally, she admitted, "that phase of my life is over." After accomplishing this, Marjorie decided to update her medical education so she could work as a professional volunteer at a community clinic. "Now, looking back on this, I think my husband did me a big favor!" she concluded.

Are you blaming others for your situation? Are you willing to stop allowing what they've done in the past to control your future? Can you forgive and get on?

REGRET: DROWNING IN PAST FAILURES

After graduating from college, Fred was a top draft choice for a major league football team. The team made it to the play-offs in his first season, and in the final game, with only moments to go, they had a last-ditch chance to come from behind and win the series title. The crucial pass came to Fred. He remembers running toward it, getting under it, certain he could catch it. He remembers having it in his hands. And then . . . it was as if his life came to a standstill. "I have replayed that moment in my mind every day of my life," he reported. Somehow, in a way that he still can't comprehend, the ball had slipped from his fingers. He heard the final buzzer and knew the game was over. His team had lost . . . and it was his fault. When we met Fred through his ex-wife, he was living in his ten-year-old Mercedes, picking up jobs here and there. His pro performance had spiraled downhill from that fated day, and within a couple of years, he'd been cut from the team. Now, at his ex-wife Celia's encouragement, he wanted to start his own business, a franchise that she believed he could get the financing to purchase, based on his name as a hometown's favorite son. He was willing, but his spirit wasn't. "Let me be candid with you," he explained. "I don't deserve any accolades. Celia is right, I've got to get myself together, but I don't want to capitalize on my short-lived fame. I let everyone down. If I'd caught that pass, well, everything would have been different. If only . . ." His words trailed off into a somber silence.

While most of us don't have such a dramatic incident to regret, remorse over things past can keep us from moving ahead. Maybe it was a career choice that didn't work out, a project we botched, a wrong decision, or an irreparable mistake. "If only . . ." I'd gone to college, gotten that scholarship, taken that job offer, stayed home with my daughter, kept trying to develop my art, followed that hunch, hadn't blown that money, hadn't gotten married to that loser, hadn't gotten divorced. You name it. Our regrets can become a lifelong punishment.

But that is not the purpose of regret. That's a misuse of this valuable emotion. Regret is designed to help us recognize the foul-ups and wrong turns in our lives. It's meant to tell us when we're off track and help us to see what we need to do differently to get back on track. But forgiveness, this time of ourselves, is the only way out of our "if only's." We must accept that we have made mistakes and that, despite these mistakes or shortcomings, we deserve to move on and give ourselves another chance at having a good life.

As Fred began to put his fateful error into perspective, he could appreciate that he was, after all, a rookie. Rookies aren't perfect. Nor, as football great Fran Tarkington can attest, are veterans. Tarkington, too, failed to complete a crucial pass in an important play-off game. But he went on throughout his career to write and speak professionally about coming back from failure and succeeding in the game of life. As Fred came to appreciate his circumstances, he could see that others had not blamed him. A game's a game. Only, he had been unable to forgive himself. If criminals can be forgiven for their crimes, he realized, surely he could forgive himself for losing a football game!

Once Fred was able to make peace with his regret, he went on to buy the franchise, as his ex-wife had suggested and, based on his name, his good standing in the community, and his determination to deliver a good service to his clients, he became a successful businessman. He also often spoke to youth groups about the role of self-forgiveness in becoming a successful person.

What are the "if only's" in your life? Are they keeping you from getting on with your life? Can you forgive yourself now for whatever you may have done in the past so you can create a new tomorrow?

One of the best things about dealing with issues like blame, regret, and resentment is the tremendous amount of energy that's freed up, once you're are no longer imprisoned by them. And, unlike many other emotions, once truly resolved, they rarely return. This is the power of acceptance and forgiveness. Saying goodbye can bring up other feelings, though, such as fear, self-doubt, and confusion. So, for more information on understanding and benefiting from any emotions that you're struggling with at this stage of changing your life, see the appendix: *A Guide to Handling the Emotions of Change.*

Having said goodbye to the past and having put it to rest, you're free to move forward with greater perspective and a more solid foundation upon which to build the future. Now it's only a matter of where to go from here.

Breakthroughs: Cloe

It was difficult for Cloe to even think about leaving the practice of law. Right from the beginning, she told the group she'd only come to the Changing Directions workshop because her husband Mark had pleaded that she accompany him. He was working in a partnership with another housing inspector and was hoping to find a new direction for his career, but he thought Cloe should, too. Reluctantly, she agreed that he was probably right. "I have no life," she admitted. "The hours on my job are very long and the pressure is very high. I've gained fifty pounds in the past five years, so I know I need to do something different, but I'm still very, very resistant to leaving law."

As the weekend progressed, Cloe pretty much held to that position. "I just can't say goodbye to all I've worked for, until I have some idea of what I'd want to say 'hello' to," she explained, resolute but nonetheless growing somewhat despondent as she heard others talking with excitement about new directions for their lives. As the last session began, she informed us that she was not yet committed to any new direction, and she waited to be the last person to comment during closing checkout.

"You will probably be surprised to learn," she reported with just a hint of a smile, "that I will be leaving the practice of law this year. I now have a new direction for my life." She was sitting next to her husband, and no one in the room could have been more surprised than he to hear this announcement. He turned to look at her, shocked and delighted, but was as much in the dark as the rest of us as to what her new direction might be.

"I've always wanted to work with Mark," she began, "b⸗
been married, we were always on our own separate c⸗
heard during this workshop that he is committed to leaving ⸗
and going into real estate development, I would like to be his busin⸗
ner and handle the legal side of the business."

At that point, her face broke into radiant smile. She was beaming as she watched Mark's mouth drop open with surprise and delight. He couldn't have been more pleased. He'd never dreamt she would be interested in partnering with him, but he looked much as we imagined he might have the night she had accepted his hand in marriage. They instinctively knew they would make a great team. Once Cloe had a glimpse of their possible new future, she had no further reservations about saying goodbye to her past.

CLOSING REFLECTION: Looking Back to Move Ahead

Think of yourself as standing at a fork in the road that is your life. Turn for a moment and look back at your life as it has been. This is the life that's changing. There is no going back to it. The road is closed. But as you look back upon it, ask yourself what you resent about that life. What do you regret? What do you appreciate? Write out your resentments, your regrets, and your appreciations in your change journal. Don't just list them abstractly or intellectually; instead, allow each of these feelings to surface as you write about them.

Read over what you've written under each category. Reflect, one by one, on their meaning for your future. What from your life is worth keeping? What needs to be eliminated? Are you willing to leave the resentments and regrets there at this crossroad in your life? Regardless of what has been done to you in the past, you deserve a future. Fold what you appreciate about your past into a small packet and put it in a special place where you can remember it.

Now, say goodbye to the life that has been your past and turn around to face your future.

If you build a dream, the dream builds you.

—MARILYN HAMILTON

FINDING YOUR WAY:

THE INNER COMPASS

Where does it come from? Who lit this flame in us
no war can put out nor conquer?
—ADAPTED FROM TERRENCE MALICK,
THE THIN RED LINE

Some of us just seem to know where to go. We're used to seeing entertainers like Madonna reinvent themselves again and again, yet even as she metamorphizes before our eyes, we all know she is still Madonna. But entertainers are not the only ones who seem to have an inner sense of who they are that enables them to change, one after another, into a wide range of seemingly different careers and lifestyles, all tied together by some inner guidance system. Former presidential candidate Bill Bradley, for example, started his career as a professional basketball player. But he has changed directions many times, going through a series of careers connected by his interest in economics and public policy. He has gone from serving eighteen years in the U.S. Senate, to advising on international business issues, to teaching at Notre Dame and Stanford, to hosting and providing political commentary on CBS and A&E Television, heading an institute, and then of course, running for president of the United States.

Football Hall of Famer Alan Page left the gridiron for a private law practice and later became chief justice of the Minnesota supreme court. Before becoming CEO of Hewlett-Packard, Carly Foirina began her career selling long-distance phone services for AT&T, shifted into manufacturing, and then specialized in applying her marketing and managerial expertise to facilitating mergers and acquisitions. Media maven Martha Stewart started out as a stockbroker, became a caterer to upscale clientele, then a stylist, a media personality, and, ultimately, the head of a multimedia empire.

What is this internal navigation system that so artfully guides these individuals from one direction to the next? And why do others seem to lack such an inner compass? When Roberta came to us, for example, she was lost. Sixteen years ago, she'd been widowed at the age of thirty-two. A stay-at-home mom with no work experience, she suddenly became the sole support of two young boys. Desperate to get a job, she, as one in four job seekers do, responded to a want ad. She got a job as a sales rep for an automotive supply company, but it wasn't an easy transition. She began working against an initial draw toward a commission—no salary. Without sales skills, Roberta had to climb her way up a steep learning curve in a male-dominated industry, but with great pride, she did learn and supported herself and her boys over the years, including sending them both to college.

Once her youngest son was about to graduate, Roberta began to think it was her turn. "I've lived my life around the boys and met my responsibilities to them. Now that I've done that, I can do whatever I want." Unfortunately, she didn't have a clue as to what that would be. She read books, listened to motivational tapes, and took career aptitude tests. "There's a lot of things I'd like to do," she confessed, but she didn't know what would be feasible at this point in her life. "I just know I don't want to sell automotive supplies anymore. I've been in survival mode all these years; now I'd like to do something that's more creative and interesting."

Ben was in a similar quandary. He'd been working, since graduation from college, as an editor with a textbook publisher. He and his wife had just purchased a new home and were about to have their second child when the publishing company he'd been working for was bought out by a New York firm. The employees were told there would be few changes under the new ownership and that they need not worry about their jobs. While some stewed, Ben was confident. "Maybe they'll lay me off, and I can write my own books for a change, instead of editing for others!" he remembers joking.

By the time we met Ben, his confidence had slipped considerably. Within weeks of the sale, the entire California office was closed and all the employees were laid off. Ben did receive a severance package though, so having those funds to draw upon, he enrolled in a professional fiction writing program and was sure that something would come along by the time he finished the program. But nothing developed, and although he enjoyed trying his hand at writing fiction, he could see it wasn't going to produce a steady income any time soon.

Ben's wife had a well-paying job, so he had some leeway. In fact, he toyed briefly with the idea of becoming a househusband and writing on the side. But between the mortgage and the new baby, he concluded that they needed two steady incomes. So, as the weeks passed, his anxiety was growing. They were falling behind on the bills and were carrying a larger credit card balance. Having been offered his editorial job right out of college through a contact from a professor, he'd never given much thought to what he wanted to do. There weren't many local editorial jobs, but he could always freelance. Or, some of his colleagues were taking jobs with Internet companies. That was hot. Maybe something could develop there. But he kept wondering, "Isn't there something more than just taking whatever job is available?" This layoff could be more than a chance to change jobs; it could be Ben's chance to "do what he loves," as the popular saying goes . . . if he just knew what that was.

Crisis had sent Roberta into a sales career. A chance referral had led Ben to a career as an editor. Neither Roberta nor Ben had any experience with designing a life or a career of their own choosing, a life that came from the inside out, instead of vice versa. But they did have an inner sense that something else was possible for them and that they should find out what it was.

Do you have a clear idea of who you are and the direction you want to go in your life? Or, like Roberta and Ben, are you not quite sure about your new direction, but just certain you want something better and more meaningful? To answer that question, ask yourself how you got on the course you've been following up until now. Was it by choice? By chance? Or by crisis?

The Task: Finding Your Passion

As we saw in the last chapter, it's easy to confuse who we are with what we do. This confusion accounts for much of the stress we experience when faced with making big changes in our lives, be they by choice, chance, or crisis. If suddenly you're stripped of your identity, it's only natural to feel adrift. Without a sense of who you are, it's hard to get your bearings and thus quite difficult to know what direction you want to head in next. But recent studies of twins are confirming what we have observed in our work over the past twenty years.

There is an intrinsic genetic element to who we are that can guide us toward the most rewarding and successful paths for our lives. If we can connect with this "inner compass," we need never feel lost, but only presented with a series of intriguing forks along the stream of our lives.

Research shows that twins reared apart share uncannily similar career and life paths. Harold and Bernard Shapiro, age sixty-four, are prime examples. Harold is president of Princeton University. His brother Bernard holds the Canadian equivalent of that position at McGill University. Their neat, orderly offices are strikingly similar, as are their career histories. They had both entered prestigious graduate schools in 1961 and chose statistical specialization—Harold in economics, Bernard in education. They both went on to become assistant professors in their fields at major universities. Later, in overlapping years, they each served as provosts. Each was then pursued by the university he now heads and had turned down its initial offers, eventually accepting second offers.

As Harold is quoted as saying in *Psychology Today,* "Something is going on here. I recognize long odds when I see them." Twin research is showing

that at least 30 percent of career satisfaction is attributable to intrinsic inner
rewards related to genetic factors, as is 50 percent of our happiness and
80 percent of our stability. Even how often and why we change careers are
partly explained by our individual nature and genetic makeup. So perhaps
we can best understand our level of satisfaction or dissatisfaction with our
circumstances in terms of how well our abilities, interests, and aptitudes
coincide with our opportunities to express them.

Some might protest that such determinism robs us of the opportunity to
shape our lives. We would argue that the opposite is true. Instead of limiting
us, such intrinsic genetic factors can serve as a reliable inner compass to
guide us, through any number of changes, to new and satisfying life choices.
There's a certain joy in doing what comes naturally and comfortably to us, a
desire to express what only we can express. And in times of rapid change,
this joy, this desire, can be a great help to us in finding our way amid a myriad of ever-changing options.

The joy that comes from pursuing your innate desires, loves, and passions
can lead you precisely where you most want to go . . . if you can listen to and
trust them.

That's the task this stage of changing directions presents to us—we must
connect with the essence of who we are so we can find the intrinsic inner
passions that will guide us naturally and easily, in a clear and satisfying new
direction. This requires doing several key things. We must first know ourselves, find what gives us joy, and then take a stand to do it.

SMILE, THAT'S YOU:
RECOGNIZING THE YOU THAT NEVER CHANGES

At first glance, we can't imagine we were ever the cuddly bare-bottomed
toddler in the family photo album or the gawky teenager smiling into the
camera before heading off at sweet sixteen to the prom. But upon a closer
look through a family photo album, we can see there is something in all the
photos of us throughout all the years that indeed is unmistakably *us*. Despite

all the changes in our appearance—our clothes, what we're doing, or where we're doing it—there remains something about each of us that makes it clear which one in the photos is us and which one isn't. This essence that shines through the years is our "identity," our true self. When we are true to this "self," we are never lost.

We flourish in circumstances where we can express our true selves. The more our interests, abilities, and creativity are recognized and encouraged, the better we feel and the clearer we become about who we are and what we want. In fact, we feel the need to change most acutely when faced with circumstances that don't allow us the freedom to express ourselves and our unfolding capabilities, interests, and desires. This is especially true when they're not only unappreciated or unrecognized but also actively discouraged, ignored, or punished.

That was certainly true for Chuck. He had always been a highly inquisitive and curious person. But when he was growing up, instead of encouraging these traits, his parents and teachers were always telling him to stop asking so many questions and pay attention to what they were telling him. But not his high school science teacher, Mr. Carlson, who appreciated Chuck's curiosity. "Keep asking questions," Carlson urged. "Science is about exploring possibilities in search of the truth, and you can't do that without asking questions."

This encouragement helped shape Chuck's interest in science and engineering, which ultimately became his career. He worked many rewarding years in the aerospace industry. But as time passed, that industry began to change. It became, from Chuck's perspective, more bureaucratic. He wasn't encouraged to push the limits anymore but was expected to simply comply with regulations and complete his projects on schedule.

At first, Chuck wasn't too bothered by this shift, but he did notice he had less interest in going to work in the morning and more interest in getting home in the evening to pursue his favorite pastime, photography. Evenings and weekends became the focus of his life as he spent them exploring and satisfying his curiosity about nature through the lens of a camera. Before long, his hobby had become so costly that, at his wife's urging, he decided to start selling some of his photographs to pay for his passion.

About that time, Chuck's job started to cramp his style. It felt like a suit jacket that was too tight to wear comfortably. "What if," he started to ponder, "I could leave this job and work full-time with my photography?" It didn't seem like a financially viable option, but he was curious about whether he could do it, so he set a goal: a full-time photography business in five years.

When the massive cuts in the aerospace programs started, Chuck was nonplussed. He knew before long, he'd probably be laid off, and secretly he was hoping he would be. His five-year goal was approaching, and he could see that if he devoted full-time to his photography, it would provide a full-time income. And so it was that by listening to the inner compass of his yearnings, Chuck was able to change directions without suffering the trauma and upheaval so many of his colleagues underwent during the collapse of the aerospace industry. After all was said and done, Chuck was still the same inquisitive, curious explorer of life's mysteries he had always been. Only the avenues for his exploration had changed, and he had engineered that change.

Who is the you that never changes? Who have you always been? What is that person hungering to do? That's your inner compass. Where would it lead if you followed its urgings?

YUM: FINDING THE SWEET LIFE

Chuck loves photography, but for him, the joy is in the opportunity it gives him to explore the intricacies of the physical world. He doesn't need a camera to do that. He has done that in his work as a scientist and as an engineer and, yes, now in his photography. Mary Ann also loves photography, but for her, the joy of it comes from something quite different. She loves to explore the richness of her subjects' inner worlds, capturing their emotions and showing the beauty of their uniqueness through her portraits. Could she do this in other ways? Of course. For several years, she did it through acting in film and theater. She has done it through interviewing those she has photographed and letting their words add to what her pictures have captured.

Soon, she will be doing it in seminars that will assist people in finding and expressing themselves through their self-image.

If you were to watch Chuck and Mary Ann at work, whether behind a camera, in the laboratory, at the drafting board, or at the podium, you would see their passion in action. You would see it in their eyes and hear in it their voices. Their work is energizing them. When they're expressing themselves through their work, life is sweet. Like everyone, they get tired, pressed, or cranky at times, but they work joyously, nonetheless, with laughter in the air. Not because of the money their work provides, although they both do earn a good living from their work, but because, much like a fine meal, their work is satisfying and rejuvenates them. It allows them to express who they are.

Where is your joy? Where is your laughter? That's your inner compass. Trust it to steer you in the right direction.

YES OR NO: PUTTING YOUR FOOT DOWN

We could hear the anger in his voice, and, yes, Gordon admitted he been flying off the handle a lot lately, upset about all kinds of things that usually don't bother him. He is the co-owner of a multimedia software company. He loves his work as a software designer. It enables him to solve intricate problems and be creative. But his partner was pressing him to finish their first major project, even though it wasn't, in Gordon's mind, ready for market. Now his wife was pressuring him, too. When, she wanted to know, would they get some income coming in? Couldn't he hurry it up so they would get paid?

He'd been going along to get along, but now his frustration was leaking out into his work and his relationships. The joy had gone out of his days. Work had become a daily round of "have to's," and neither his partner nor his wife seemed to want to hear his point of view. Something was going to have to change. He knew who he was at heart—a creative problem solver— and he knew that's what gave him joy and satisfaction. But he was indecisive about his situation. Should he split off from his partner and do the project on his own? Should he turn over the project to his partner and take a job where he could work at a more reasonable pace? Or should he just turn in the project they wanted him to do and hope things would go better on the next project?

Gordon had lost his sense of direction. He wasn't connected to his inner compass. He felt powerless against his wife's and his partner's impassioned insistence that he simply patch things together and ship the product off as is. And, of course, the more inflexible they became, the more inflexible he felt. It seemed like it was either him or them.

But as Gordon began to talk out his situation, his confusion began to clear. He was not willing to send out a shoddy product. That's not who he was. He believed in the original idea they had conceived and wanted to take the time to create it as they had conceived it. When he expressed this conviction clearly to his partner and his wife, with a newfound sense of confidence, they got the message. Gordon and his partner requested, and obtained, an extension on the due date. Meanwhile, based on an amended contract, Gordon was able to obtain a line of credit, which eased his wife's financial concerns. Having the clarity to put his foot down gave him the ability to inspire the confidence of others and the flexibility to see new options.

As with Chuck and Gordon, the key to finding *your* way is to:

1. Know who you are
2. Know what gives you joy
3. Know what you do and don't want, and what you will and won't do

This inner knowing is our inner compass. It tells us when we're on track and when we're not, when to stick it out and when to head off in a new direction . . . if we listen. By listening, Chuck began investing more time in his avocation well before he had to. By listening, Gordon hesitated before sending out his product without assuring it was the best it could be.

When Jonathon Storm listened to his inner voice, he knew he must leave architectural school to apprentice as a nature-recording artist and start his own recording studio. When MBA graduate Ann Christie Gusliff listened to her inner compass, she abandoned her plans to become a corporate executive and decided to use her business expertise to launch, Clothes the Deal, a nonprofit organization devoted to providing suitable business attire to homeless job applicants. Nightclub owner Joseph Brooks had forgotten what made him happy until he listened. He'd always loved bird watching, but for years the only birds he watched were on the Discovery Channel. Then, a dying friend reminded him, "Don't waste your life." He now spends his time crisscrossing the globe, sketching exotic birds and leading bird-watching tours for children.

What change in direction is your inner compass suggesting for you?

TURBO FUEL: Connecting with Your Inner Compass

In the crush of life's changing expectations and demands, it's easy to lose touch with our inner navigational system. We can forget who we are at heart and stop listening to our desires. If we do this long enough, we don't even remember what will give us joy, and we become confused about what we want and what we don't. But even when you've forgotten these things, you do know them, and the following process will help you to remember.

Set aside at least half an hour when you can arrange not to be interrupted. Write out your responses to the following queries in your change journal. If you are working through this book with a partner or a group, this is an excellent process to do together. Set aside half an hour for each person. Take one person through the entire process at a time. Have someone in the group ask the following questions, using the precise words below. Do not alter the way the queries are worded. Have others in the group take notes so each person will have a record of what they've described.

By a particular experience or event we mean a specific, distinct occurrence or incident. Be sure to describe each experience *in detail*.

Example:
Not: *"I love birthday parties."*

Not: "*One of my favorite experiences was my best friend's birthday party two years ago.*"

Instead: "*I planned a surprise party for my best friend's birthday two years ago while she was recovering from breast cancer. She had no idea I was doing this and never even suspected. I arranged for everyone she loved to be there with her, even friends and family from out of town. I prepared her favorite foods and played her favorite music. When she walked through the door and saw us all there for her, she cried tears of joy and we all cried with her and sang and danced to the music. . . . etc.*"

Not: "*It was meaningful.*"

Not: "*What I liked about that was how appreciative she was.*"

Instead: "*What I liked about that was being able to bring such joy to someone whose friendship had given me so much joy. That I am able to understand her needs and who she is well enough to know what she would appreciate. That I could orchestrate all the activities and have them come together in perfect harmony. That I created a magical moment many people will never forget . . . etc.*"

Now it's your turn:

1. Describe in detail one of your favorite work experiences, a particular experience or event.

     What did you like about that?

2. Describe in detail another of your favorite work experiences, a particular experience or event.

     What did you like about that?

3. Describe in detail a favorite experience in your life unrelated to work, a specific event.

     What did you like about that?

4. Describe in detail another favorite experience in your life unrelated to work, a particular experience or event.

     What did you like about that?

5. Sit quietly and read back through all your responses. Identify the core themes that run through the experiences you described. (If you are

doing this as a group, everyone should quietly review their notes.) These core themes are at the heart of who you are, and they are an expression of your inner compass. They are your personal essence in action.

6. Look for words, patterns, feelings, and images you've used repeatedly that suggest common themes within your favorite experiences.

Underline or use a colored highlighter to identify common terms, themes, etc., that run throughout the descriptions. (If you're doing this as a group, everyone should contribute to this list, beginning with the person who is responding.)

7. Summarize your essence or inner compass, based on your observations of common themes, by completing this sentence:

"I am a man/woman who naturally. . . ."

8. Now, as a check, describe in detail one of your favorite childhood experiences, a particular experience or event.

What did you like about that?

Does it provide a feeling that's similar to the other experiences you described?

9. Describe another of your favorite childhood experiences, a particular experience or event.

What did you like about that?

Does it provide a feeling that is similar to the other experiences you described?

10. Describe the feeling that runs through all these experiences and allow yourself to feel that feeling fully. Then associate a color with that feeling. Does it have a form or shape? Is there a scene taking place around it? This is your inner compass.

11. Once you have completed this process, draw or find some material object that represents your inner compass. Carry this object with you or put it where you will see it often.

Paying attention to the feelings you have identified through this process will guide you in a fulfilling and satisfying new direction for your life. It's like a barometer. When what you're doing or considering provides this feeling, you're heading along a path that's allied with your inner compass. If this feeling is consistently absent from what you're doing or considering, you're heading away from the direction your inner compass would guide you toward.

SAMPLE INNER COMPASS SYNOPSIS: AN ACTRESS

1. A favorite work experience, a particular experience or event: "An episode of the TV series I was in where my character had a story line. It was a **huge responsibility** and **very hard work,** which I **accomplished without a problem.** I was very happy and proud of the results.

"What I liked about it was that I was **under pressure** and I not only **performed well,** but the work was **very honest and true.** It was **exhilarating.**"

2. A second favorite work experience, a particular experience or event: "In New York, I played Roselind in a Shakespearean company performance of As You Like It *and I was able to* **lose myself** *in the role.* **Very honest and true work.**

"What I liked about it was that I felt like **a consummate actor.** I **served the play** and was **completely in character.** It was a **very tough job** and it **felt so easy** for me."

3. A favorite experience in your life unrelated to work, a particular experience or event: "Giving birth to my son. I was in labor for **47½ hours** with no drugs and I **overcame physical problems** to have a natural birth.

"What I liked about that was I **did the best thing** for my son, even though it was **hard** for me. He has been the best thing in my life."

4. A second favorite experience in your life unrelated to work, a particular experience or event: "My wedding day. It was a beautiful ceremony and a loving day. Handling all the various personalities and their needs was **a lot of responsibility, very challenging** as there were some

difficult family issues, but I was able to **handle it without diminish-
ing the joy** of the day.

"What I liked about it was that I was finally able to be intimate and
trust someone enough to **love unconditionally** and allow someone to
love me fully."

5. *Highlight core themes which run through these experiences that
express your inner compass, your essence in action. (See underlined
words and phrases above.)*

6. *Common words, patterns, feelings, and images:* handling difficult,
very challenging responsibilities easily and successfully. Doing the best
thing for everyone. Being honest and true. Serving the situation. Losing
and giving self fully and completely to what's required.

7. *Summary:* "I am a woman who naturally gives myself fully to what I
do. I find challenge and difficulty exhilarating. I like to do my best with
truth, honesty, and integrity and can follow that course, even in adver-
sity. I don't take the easy way out."

8. *A favorite childhood experience, a particular experience or event:* "I
loved role-playing different characters and adventures with my cousin
and our dolls.

"What I liked about that was the closeness with my cousin and the
fantasy of creating a character and disappearing into a role.

"Is that the same feeling? Yes, abandoning my ego, the transformational experience of becoming someone else."

9. *A second favorite childhood experience, a particular experience or
event:* "When I was chosen to perform in Barefoot in the Park in high
school. It was my first time on stage. I was making people laugh.

"What I liked about that was the transformational experience. I
loved the audience enjoying me. It was an escape for me and for them,
taking us both into a new experience.

"Is that the same feeling? Yes. The same exhilaration. The same sense of rising to challenge and the sense of stepping out of my ego.

10. *"The color of that feeling is gold, like sunshine. It does have a form. It's like a spotlight. It fills the room and touches everyone with its light."*

11. *Object: "It reminds me of the diamond pendant my husband gave me for our wedding anniversary. I've always loved it and virtually never take it off. It represents that feeling for me."*

Do you remember Bonnie? She was trying to change jobs but was blocked by association with her father's bad experiences in following his dreams. Well, Bonnie had an interesting experience when she did her Inner Compass process. Usually, there is a thread of similarity that runs along all the favorite memories—work-related, personal, and childhood. That thread is the Inner Compass. But sometimes, as in Bonnie's case, there is no thread between certain memories.

Her work-related memories were about feeling good after completing projects and getting praise for solving problems for her boss. Her nonwork and childhood memories, however, were about experiences she had out of doors, especially related to the sea and interacting with animals. The contrast was dramatic. "I think I've lost track of my inner compass in my career," she commented.

Perhaps you can relate to Bonnie's initial disbelief that she could bring the wonderful feelings she'd had in childhood into her work. But she could quickly see how deciding to adopt her mother's practicality had cut her off from such possibilities.

When we asked her what type of work could provide that feeling, she immediately knew it would involve working outdoors with animals. This realization ultimately led to her deciding to become a marine mammal trainer.

Are there areas of your life where you're disconnected from your Inner Compass? How did that happen? How can you reconnect?

Being able to recognize the feeling associated with your Inner Compass is the first step to feeling grounded and guided, even in the most unsettling of situations. The next step is to make sure you pay attention to the guidance you're getting. The following questions will help you know when you're listening and when you're not.

Are You Listening?

Are you tuned in to your inner compass, or are you allowing outdated beliefs and limiting fears and doubts direct the course of your life? Whenever you catch yourself saying or thinking any of the following statements, you are not listening to your inner compass and are instead sabotaging your efforts to fulfill your desires.

To reconnect with your inner compass and get your life back on track, replace these self-defeating thoughts with the suggested affirmations that follow them in italic. We're using the term *affirmation* to mean declarations or assertions of intention. Once you've worked through whatever feelings are preventing you from believing these affirmations, you'll be able to hear what your inner compass is saying.

Check any of the following statements that apply to you and be attuned to intercept them whenever they arise.

- "I'm bored." Boredom is usually a sign that you're doing what someone else wants you to do, not what you want to do. It's a sure sign you're not listening to your inner compass.
  AFFIRMATION: *What's most important to me guides my life, and I pursue it with enthusiasm.*
- "I shouldn't feel this way." Knowing what you feel and allowing yourself to feel and express it appropriately is the only way to discover and clarify what you want, and what is and is not best for you.
  AFFIRMATION: *"My feelings are important. I listen to understand what they mean to me and find ways to express them instead of avoiding them."*

- "There's nothing I'm really passionate about." We all have dreams in our hearts born from desire. Passion is a strong desire, and it's what shows us the best way to head and energizes and motivates us to keep going through life's ups and downs. We only know what we really want by listening to our desires.

  AFFIRMATION: *It's okay for me to find joy in life.*

- "But this is what I have to do." Until you can stand up for what you want to do, you will always end up doing what others want you to do.

  AFFIRMATION: *"I effectively define and express what I want and only agree to do what I really want to do."*

- "What's the use? There's nothing I can do about it." Those who are successful in life are the ones who do the hard work others aren't willing to do. They know where there's a will, there's a way.

  AFFIRMATION: *"I can have what I want in life. I can figure out and do what it takes to get it."*

- "Yes, But what if . . . ?" We can't explore the possibilities our inner compass provides if our minds are filled with constant worry and concern about what could happen. Like a butterfly, new yearnings and novel possibilities need the time and space to unfold before we can see their potential take form.

  AFFFIRMATON: *"I approach the possibilities and problems in my life with curiosity. I wonder what would work. I ask, how could I do it?"*

Hung Up? Getting through
Stage Three

There are many ways to tune out our inner compass without even knowing we have. If you know you need to change and you're ready to make a change but you're not taking steps to make it or making any progress toward it, it's a sure sign you're not tuned in. Without an inner navigation system to guide us on, we either reach a standstill or we move on aimlessly without a sense of where we're headed or why. Here are three of the most common logjams to getting through this stage and how to break through them.

TRAUMA: WRITTEN OFF AS PIPE DREAMS

If you recall, Roberta had been selling automotive supplies since her husband died, leaving her with two young sons to raise. Once they had graduated from college, she was ready to say goodbye to her job and hello to a new life, but her question was, Doing what? There were so many exciting possibilities, she felt like a kid in a candy shop. But from doing the Inner Compass process, the direction was clear. Her favorite experiences were all related to her love of arts and crafts and her memories from happier days when she was married.

She had come from a creative family. Her mother was an artist, her father an architect. Before her husband's death, she spent whatever free time she had in the little art studio she'd created in a sunny corner of their attic. She and her husband, an art dealer, spent many weekends wheeling baby strollers through art galleries and the aisles of outdoor arts-and-crafts fairs. At these fairs, Roberta realized she had an uncanny knack for recognizing emerging talent. She often purchased the early works of unknown artists who quickly went on to develop a devoted following.

Reflecting on these times, she felt sad that there had been so little creativity in her life for so many years, so we began brainstorming for ideas of possible careers in arts and crafts. We came up with a wealth of creative options, from working as a rep for talented new artists to creating online web site galleries for artists or planning and leading art tours. As we discussed each of these ideas, Roberta's energy level rose markedly. Her voice became more animated. Her eyes lit up with excitement. "Are you having that inner compass feeling?" we asked. Her reply was a resounding yes! She was elated with the prospects she was considering and set off to do some research on the details of creating a new life in the art world.

But her mood soon shifted. She'd been "taking care of business," as she put it, for so long that doing something she wanted to do seemed frivolous and impractical, especially given the way she'd been feeling. She'd been chronically tired for years. But that, she had always assured herself, was understandable: she was a single mom. Now with fewer responsibilities, her fatigue, instead of abating, was getting worse, and she was worried she might have some kind of serious health problem her doctors couldn't identify, maybe something like chronic fatigue or fibromyalgia. How could she possibly go off in pursuit of some pipedream like working with artists? It was just too speculative, too unpredictable. Just the thought of it gave her a headache. She might lose the little security she'd built for herself over all these years.

So, after some consideration, she decided to settle back into her sales job. At least there she was in control, and although she continued to dislike the job, she would probably have stayed there indefinitely had providence not intervened. Roberta developed a severe case of hypoglycemia and had to go on disability for several months. While flat on her back day after day, resting for the first time in over a decade, the years of grief and disappointment she'd suffered finally broke through. She cried for days. She cried for the loss of her husband, something she'd never had time to do. Even at the funeral, for the boys' sake, she'd had been dry-eyed. She cried for the years of financial struggle she'd endured. She cried for the creativity she'd lost to the drudgery of making endless cold calls. Then, gradually she began to feel better.

"I realized," she explained, "I was so afraid something terrible might happen to me again that I would have done anything to avoid losing what I'd built. Every time I thought about the exciting things we talked about, I would just shut down." The trauma of Roberta's past had blinded her to the potential of her future. While on disability, however, as her strength grew, she began to surf art sites on the Web and then started attending a few art fairs. Her strength grew, as she renewed her love for art, and soon she was making contact with undiscovered artists whose work caught her eye. A growing number of them were eager for Roberta's help in marketing their work. She was following her inner compass, and her life was taking on a new direction.

Have you written your dreams off as pipe dreams, for fear of repeating some past or imagined trauma? Can you see how the present is different from your past, or how it could be if you made it so?

NO HEAT: FROZEN IN A PASSIONLESS PIT

While Roberta had many options but feared selecting any one of them, Gloria saw no options . . . at least no desirable ones. Like many people we receive e-mail from, Gloria wanted to break out of a rut. She'd been in a dead-end administrative job for years but hadn't made a change because, frankly, there wasn't anything that looked any better to her. Like Roberta, she'd read books and taken aptitude tests, but when it came to finding her passion, everything she considered left her cold. But our Inner Compass process provided an interesting insight.

Her favorite experiences were related to detailed memories of times when her children were having fun. Her favorite childhood memories were times when her mother was having fun. "But what about you?" we asked. "When do you have fun?" Unfortunately, she drew a blank. As we discussed various things she was considering doing with her life, the conversation was peppered with comments like "Well, that wouldn't be too bad," "I could put up with that," and "I won't mind this too much."

Exploring further, we discovered that Gloria, an only child, grew up in a strict Germanic family. Her father was a comptroller and a brigadier general in the military reserves. There was no laughter in their house, at least not when he was home. Everything was expected to kept spic-and-span and orderly at all times. Gloria wasn't allowed to play outside when it rained or snowed, because she would track in too much dirt. Nor could she bring friends over to play. They would create too much of a mess.

Gloria's mother was a closet alcoholic and was often passed out on the couch when Gloria got home from school. "I used to think my mother was taking a nap," she remembered. "I had to be really quiet when I came in because Mother would be really angry if I disturbed her 'nap.'" Later, of course, Gloria realized it was more than fatigue that put her mother on the couch.

But if Gloria had been real quiet and gotten everything cleaned up and in order around the house before her father got home, sometimes her mother would be quite cheerful when she woke up. Then they would bake cookies, pies, cakes, or fudge for the evening's dessert, and her mother would laugh and sing while cooking. Those were her favorite times. In fact, Gloria still does a lot of baking when she gets home from work, and, as a result, her whole family is overweight. "We should cut back on sweets," she confessed, "but you've got to have at least one indulgence."

Are you having a difficult time deciding what you would love to do? Is it hard for you to identify your passion?

It was no wonder Gloria had no idea how she wanted to change her life; having spent her entire life pleasing others and doing what was expected of her, she'd put up with so many things she didn't like that she'd never had the chance to discover what *she* would like. Gloria couldn't define what her interests were, because she'd never developed any. When family and friends asked Gloria what she wanted to do for an evening's entertainment, she would automatically reply, "Well, what would you like to do?" If they asked how she liked a particular movie, her response would be, "What did you think of it?" When asked, "How are you doing?" she always said, "I'm fine" or "Could be worse."

Gloria was surprised to discover these habits were not only keeping her stuck in a rut but also were driving her family crazy. They wanted her to define what she felt and what she wanted. In order to recognize her own preferences, though, Gloria had to begin with the basics. Did she prefer to shower or take a bath? Did she like to sleep with the window open or closed? She'd never thought about things like these before. Growing up in her household, everyone took showers because it was more efficient. Everyone also slept with the window open because that's what her father liked. To discover what she liked or didn't like, Gloria had to try out a lot of new things so she could compare them with the way she'd always done them before. Her new motto became, "Try it, you might like it." She soon discovered, among other things, that she preferred baths and sleeping in a warm room.

Gloria also had to accept that what she liked wouldn't always be what the significant others in her life liked, and she would have to take a stand for her preferences. This was especially hard because she didn't want to offend, disappoint, displease, or bother anyone. Gradually, she noticed that she had many different preferences. For example, while her husband loved pickles, she didn't, and from the day of that realization she stopped putting them on her plate! Before long, she found her first passion: comedies. She loved to laugh.

Not long after that, Gloria began to notice that there were things about her work as an administrative assistant that she really liked. She loved organizing things, for example, and was very good at it (she'd mastered it in childhood). But she hated taking phone calls and keeping financial records. Most of all, she hated being taken for granted and being paid a pittance for her efforts. So she started looking for what she would enjoy and be appreciated for and found something she had a real enthusiasm for—professional organizing. It was a natural for her.

TURBO FUEL: Following the Compass

If you find you have a hard time knowing what you want to do next in your life, try this:

Set aside an afternoon or morning when you have absolutely nothing scheduled and no one else's agenda to contend with. Then, allow your inner compass to fill the time. Do whatever comes to your mind. Follow your whims. If you feel like going back to bed, do so. If you feel like watching a soap opera, do so. If you feel like calling an old friend, going to a movie, surfing the Web, digging in the garden, puttering in the attic, whatever—do it until you want to do something else. If nothing comes to mind, do nothing until something does.

Then, write in your Change Journal about this experience. How did it feel to follow your inner compass? What thoughts and feelings came up? What did you learn about yourself? What did you enjoy? What didn't you enjoy? What would you want to do again?

To learn more about your likes and dislikes, extend this exercise to a day or to a weekend. Try new things you're curious about or drawn to. Make a habit of setting aside time to follow your compass; you may be surprised at what you've discovered.

PASSIVITY: WAITING FOR A WAVE

While Roberta got stuck fearing to choose among several appealing options and Gloria got stuck by seeing no appealing options, Ben, the San Diego editor who had been laid off, knew exactly what he wanted to do but was stuck because he wouldn't admit it. The Inner Compass process brought his real desires into the open and forced him to face the reason that he always seemed to settle for less than what he wanted.

Ben's favorite experiences all centered around a combination of three things: literature, physical exercise, and the pastoral countryside of northern Italy. He loved hiking or biking around northern Italy, which he and his wife had done every summer vacation. In fact, both fluent in Italian, they had met and fallen in love on a trip to Italy and had been married there. He found the Italian countryside both exhilarating and inspiring, and reminiscent of his favorite childhood experiences visiting his grandfather's farm in the valley near Aspen.

When we pointed out how little his work as an editor resembled these favorite experiences, he confessed what he'd always wanted to do: organize retreats for U.S. writers to Italian villas where they could spend a season relaxing, biking, hiking, and honing their writing skills. "That is a great idea!" we exclaimed. What a perfect match between his experience, skills, and passions and how timely, with the recent best-selling books on Italy! "But I can't do that!" he gasped. "How would that ever happen?"

And that was the problem. It was a grand and feasible idea, but it would never "happen." Everything in Ben's life just happened. He came from a comfortable middle-class family who paved the way for him through the right schools and charted his success through graduation from college. Then, a favorite literature professor, who had become Ben's mentor, paved the way into an editorial career. On the professor's recommendation, the textbook publisher, who Ben had worked for since graduating, recruited him with an invitation to lunch. Recognizing Ben's talent, the publisher had taken him under his wing and steered Ben up the ranks to a senior editor position.

But no one was going to invite Ben to organize and run writers' retreats in northern Italy. No wonder he couldn't see that happening. For that to happen, Ben would have to take the initiative to make it happen. So, yes, as Ben had been wondering, there was something more to life than settling for whatever was available, but not if he kept waiting for something to come along. Already he felt pressed to take whatever he could. He would have to choose between the constraints of what was available or the freedom of what he could create. Much of what he loves so much about Italy (and his grandfather's farm) is how free he feels there. "There's plenty of room there for me to breathe," he said, taking a long, deep breath as he remembered the feeling. It was his inner-compass feeling. To follow it he would have to imagine how he could do it. He took another deep breath. He wanted to do it. He couldn't wait to begin exploring the possibilities.

TURBO FUEL: Release Your Breath and Free Your Imagination

All action, as distinguished from reaction, begins with a deep breath. Oxygen fuels our muscles. Breath carries our words to the world. It enables us to be proactive, to initiate. And, of course, it's always at our command. But when we're tense, pressed, or worried, we tend to hold our breath, depriving ourselves of precisely what we need most to get moving. Here's a quick way to relax, release your breath, and free your imagination:

Close your eyes and look up at a bright light. Sunlight is preferable but a bright indoor light will suffice, if necessary. Let the light shine in through your eyelids (don't open your eyes) for a minute or two. Then lower your head, open your eyes, and look over your right shoulder. Focus on whatever you see there for another minute and then repeat the process, but this time look over your left shoulder after soaking in the light.

Once you've found your inner compass, it's always there to help guide your journey into the future and help you discover where to go next.

Breakthrough: Mark

"I've pretty much lost my direction," Mark admitted, in introducing himself to the Changing Directions group seminar. For the past five years, he'd been doing housing inspection with a partner he met in the army reserves. While this produced a decent enough income for him, for the past three years, the work had felt routine and dull. He'd fallen into it after returning from the Gulf War, only to discover the housing construction market was off. "I'd been an architectural draftsman and I loved my work. It was the best. I love the housing industry, but there's just no joy in this work. I just can't seem to find my niche now. So my partner and I want to expand the business, hire other inspectors, and spend our time managing the company instead of doing the work."

Mark had come with the intention of getting help in developing a strategy for this change, and although he didn't seem particularly ecstatic about it, he was convincing enough that we all felt confident that he was clear and committed to his new direction. But the results of his Inner Compass process surprised him, and he surprised us all when, toward the close of the weekend, he announced he was making a major change in his plans. "I won't find managing an inspection company any more fulfilling than doing inspections. I'm not a detail-oriented person," he explained. "I'm a big picture guy. I like to delegate, but I want to do something that involves a lot of challenge. I want to create something big and original."

He remembered how he'd always imagined what it would be like to be the developer of the housing projects he was drafting. He'd even brought up the idea to his partner of their doing real estate development together and had taken some real estate courses, but his partner never cared much for the idea. Now, Mark wasn't going to even try to convince his partner to go in this new direction with him. "I feel connected to something again," he told us. "I'm going to sell my half of the inspection business and start doing what I want to do."

Little did Mark know at the moment that by declaring this, he would soon have not only a new direction but also a new partner, his wife Cloe.

CLOSING REFLECTION

Take a moment to recall your inner-compass feeling. Let that feeling build. Then, ask yourself, "If I could take my life in any direction whatsoever, what would it be? If I could do anything with my life, what would I do?" Avoid any temptation to censor your responses. Write them in your Change Journal. Notice any feelings you have as you do this reflection. Should any thoughts arise like the ones listed above that keep you from listening to your inner compass, note them. What will you have to face about yourself, your past, your habits, and your ways of operating if you are to allow yourself to do what your yearning to do? What will you need to do differently? Are you willing to change so you can follow your inner compass?

> *What has not burst forth from your own soul*
> *will never refresh you.*
>
> —GOETHE

Stage Four

SAYING HELLO TO WHERE YOU'RE GOING: EMBRACING THE FUTURE

Life is too short to wait to live a memorable life.
—JEANNE MOORE

Dorothea made the one mistake people most often make when they try to take charge of their lives. She'd put in twenty-five years in the art department of a large insurance company, but for the past five years she had been counting down the days to a generous early retirement package. When the day finally came, she was only forty-six-years old, and, just as planned, she and her husband Clifford moved across the state to a fast-growing suburban area to be near their grandchildren. There, at last, Dorothea thought, she would have time to do what she'd always wanted to do—create illustrated children's books.

Her new life started out well enough. She set up a loft with ample natural light where she could work undisturbed. It was well away from Clifford's office downstairs where he ran a small advertising agency, so they could work without disrupting each other. But they often took off for lunch together or for an afternoon round of golf. Weekends were usually spent with their kids and grandchildren. Dorothea was beginning to believe she'd found the happiness she'd been waiting for. But in her enthusiasm for her newfound freedom, she began steadily sabotaging her own plans.

First, her daughter wanted to go back to graduate school for a degree in counseling and wanted Dorothea to watch the kids while she was in class. Dorothea was delighted to help. She had missed being able to be a real grandmother while she was working. Then, Clifford was easing his way into a semiretirement, so he decided not to hire a new administrative assistant. Since Dorothea had always hoped that someday she and Clifford would work together, she offered to help him with invoicing and bookkeeping. He also needed some graphic design work done, so to save the cost of hiring an outside service to do the work, she volunteered to do that, too.

Dorothea wanted to enjoy everything she'd missed out on while working full-time, but, instead, her new life was starting to feel like her old one, devoid of time for herself. She began having headaches and difficulty sleeping. She'd wake up in the middle of the night feeling tense and unable to get back to sleep. "It can't be old age," she joked. "I'm not old enough for that! What's wrong? I should be having the time of my life!"

Dorothea had lost her focus. She was spreading herself too thin. Instead of focusing on what was most important to her at this point in her life, which was to relax, enjoy her family, and start creating illustrated children's books, she was trying to be everything to everyone.

Don nearly made a similar mistake. When the commercial architectural firm he was associated with disbanded, he panicked. He knew business had been off, but he hadn't confronted the reality of the situation until the vote to disband came up. Since he'd always wanted to be more independent, his first thought was that this was his chance to go solo. But with business being off, how could he make it on his own? At a friend's urging, he considered buying a sign-making franchise. Commercial architecture, sign-making: they seemed similar. He could enjoy doing either business and had the skills to do them both. If he could get the sign-making business going, he figured, it would provide just enough extra income to launch a solo architectural practice.

But Don was hesitant. Something was eating at him. What if he put the little extra money he had into this sign business and it didn't work out? He would be even further behind the eight ball financially. As he examined his concerns with us, he realized that to succeed in his own architectural firm, he would need to focus on a residential clientele, because the commercial market was too weak. That's why his firm had disbanded. But he would be selling signs to a commercial market. That would be like starting up two entirely different new businesses: exhausting, expensive, and confusing to those who would want to know what business he was in.

Don realized he would have to make a choice—architecture or sign-making? After checking in with his inner compass and doing some financial projections, he decided to pass on the sign-making business. But that left him with a new dilemma: how would he establish himself in the competitive world of residential architecture? Lots of other financially strapped architects were headed there, too.

Valerie faced a similar dilemma. She was working as an administrative assistant when a painful degenerative disc disease prompted her doctor to suggest that she get more exercise. Valerie headed to the gym, and after sticking to a regimen of resistance training, yoga, and aerobic exercise, she was pain-free and had discovered a new passion. She was in love with fitness and wanted to devote her life to teaching people how it could change their lives. But how could she, with no experience except her own personal transformation, get a toe in the competitive field of health and fitness? It seemed like an overwhelming task . . . until she had an idea.

Valerie could focus her fitness program on helping companies educate their administrative personnel about how exercise, posture, nutrition, movement, and breathing could prevent or correct work-related injuries and help these employees become more energetic, creative, and productive. This, she hypothesized, would be her niche, combining fitness and ergonomics—"the science of fitting jobs to workers."

With varying degrees of success, Dorothea, Don, and Valerie were each dealing with the next inevitable challenge of changing directions—knowing in what direction you want to go and committing yourself to going there. In other words, it's decision time, time to identify *one* clear direction that fits both with what you want to do in life and with the realities of what you can do, given your existing situation. Time to choose a specific direction you can devote your available energy and resources toward.

How clear are you about where you're headed next? Do you have one clear direction you want to take? Or are you trying to go in several directions at once?

The Task: Committing to a Focus

Changing directions is much like deciding where to go on vacation. Some people have a favorite place in mind and are fortunate enough to have both the means and the opportunity to get there. For them, vacation planning is a breeze. They know where they're going, so all they have to do is make the reservations, pack, and show up on time. But before most of us can decide to go on vacation, we need to explore various possibilities, weigh the options, and fit our travel plans into our lives, our budgets, and what we're actually up for doing.

We may want to go to Paris but have a budget for the Ozarks. We might want to tour Australia but only have enough time off for a long weekend in New York. The idea of going on an African safari may sound intriguing until we discover what's involved; then we may realize we feel more like taking a Hawaiian cruise. Still, if we're going to take a vacation before the year's out, we've got to make a decision. Like it or not, we can't go to Paris, New York, and Hawaii at the same time.

So it is with changing directions. If we're going to get somewhere in life, we have to make choices. We have to focus or flail. Just as we can't develop a travel itinerary until we know our destination, we can't develop a strategy until we've found a focus. We must survey the land, take a reading with our inner compass, and make a choice that fits with our lifestyle, our budget, and our inclinations.

MAKE ROOM: FINDING A FIT

As you recall, Dorothea's life had been out of balance for many years. It had revolved around working and saving for early retirement. She had wanted to be more involved with her children and grandchildren. She had wanted to work with her husband. She had wanted to illustrate children's books. She had wanted to have the time to relax, travel, and play golf. So when she finally reached her goal of early retirement, she rushed eagerly into doing it all, only to find herself just as overwhelmed as when she was working a full-time job.

According to the U.S. Department of Labor, the one difficulty expressed most often by both men and women is trying to balance all the demands of work and family. Most of our lives are severely overstuffed and out of balance. We feel like we have way too much to do and way too little time to do it in. Yet, if our lives are to be satisfying, we must find a balance. We need time for meaningful work that pays for a good life. We need time for family and loved ones. And we need time to relax and enjoy ourselves.

The struggle with finding balance is one reason many of us have a hard time committing to a clear focus for our future. We want to do work we enjoy, but we need to earn a living. We want a certain level of material comfort, but we also want the time to enjoy it. So, sometimes it takes a lot of wiggling and jiggling around to fit everything into our lives comfortably. Sometimes, an uncomfortable fit is what's propelling us to make a change in the first place. Other times, everything in our lives was fitting just fine until changes in our circumstances forced us or, as in Dorothea's case, enticed us, into a change that doesn't fit as well.

TURBO FUEL: The Time Pie

Think of your life as a pie that must feed three hungry children: yourself, the important others in your life, and the worker who supports all of you. Is everyone getting their share of your time, money, and energy? To find out, subtract the number of hours you usually sleep from the twenty-four hours in a day and then reflect on how many of those remaining hours you spend working? How many are spent with important others? How many are spent relaxing and enjoying yourself?

Of course, some activities may overlap, but don't fool yourself. That's what Dorothea was doing. That's what her headaches and insomnia were trying to tell her. Just because you like your job or your family, this doesn't necessarily mean the time you invest in them is time invested in your own needs.

Yes, Dorothea enjoyed helping her husband and, yes, she enjoyed being with her grandbabies, but her personal goals were getting short shrift. She wasn't getting the enjoyment from retirement she'd expected. She and her husband were working instead of finding time to golf together. She was baby-sitting instead of working in the studio on her illustrations. Her pie had gone from being overcommitted to work, to being overcommitted to others:

Dorothea's Imbalanced Past   **Dorothea's Imbalanced Present**

Draw a time pie of your life as it is now and as you'd like it to be. Draw a pie for the various alternative futures you're considering. If you don't know enough about the options you're considering to know the time implications, do some homework and interview others who are traveling a similar path. Are they balancing the various aspects of their life comfortably? Could you do what they're doing? Would you want to? Or are your circumstances sufficiently different from theirs?

ADD IT UP: PAYING THE WAY

Don's dilemma, if you recall, was that he had to choose between purchasing a sign franchise or setting up his own architectural practice, or both. Initially, he thought he would do both. But when Don told us about the sign franchise, the conversation was factual, practical, and clear; there was no light in his eyes, no excitement in his voice. Conversation about starting his own practice was an entirely different experience. As he spoke about going solo, he became animated and energized. It was clearly a reflection of his inner compass. So why had Don put so much effort into deciding on two businesses to invest his time, money, and energy in when only one was lighting his fire? The answer was, of course, money.

Worry and concern about whether they can make enough money is the number-one reason people don't find and commit to a clear focus. Instead, they hedge their bets and make compromises in hopes of creating a financial safety net. But usually such compromises become financial drains instead. As Don realized, had he tried to launch two divergent businesses at once, he would have been spreading his limited resources too thin. He needed what we all need—one clear direction that he could commit himself to wholeheartedly.

Finding that focus requires making a match between where your inner compass is urging you to go and what people will pay you to do. We call this matchmaking process *matrixing*. It refers to finding where your interests, skills, talents, resources, and desired lifestyle overlap with what people need and will pay for. Your niche lies at this overlap. That's where you can shine.

Valerie's focus on educating company employees about the powerful combination of fitness and ergonomics is an excellent example of effective matrixing because, while she doesn't yet know everything she needs to succeed, she has

- a passion for doing it
- experience and firsthand knowledge of it
- an eagerness to learn more
- a service that companies need and will pay for to keep their insurance costs and absenteeism down
- a growing number of contacts in the worlds of business, medicine, and fitness

Over the years of helping people redirect their lives, we've been amazed by the unique, intriguing, interesting, and delightfully successful ways people have been able to matrix their heart's desires with real-world realities. Often, it's not in spite of their circumstances that they find such a great match, but because of them. Here are just a few examples from our book *Finding Your Perfect Work*:

- Actress Chellie Campbell combined her experience as a bookkeeper and her passion for performing with her desire to free people from financial distress in order to create the popular Financial Stress Reductions seminars.
- Eileen Lizer combined her extraordinary photographic memory, her love for tracking down information, and her experience booking guests on a popular radio talk show into the brand-new field of "findology." She tracks down unusual and obscure information and resources her clients need.
- After spending a lifetime taking care of others, sixty-something Bette Perry combines her boundless energy, her passion for life, and her wide range of unusual work experiences—from driving a tank to styling hair, farming and payroll clerking—into a successful career as a motivational comedian.
- George Alistair matrixed his passion for video games, his quirky personality, musical talent, and experience in marketing into a career creating musical soundtracks for interactive multimedia computer games.
- When Barbara Lambert wanted to find work that involved less travel, she drew upon her sales experience as the first female auctioneer in Georgia, her love for doing research, and her background in collecting art, to become a video detective, tracking down, buying, selling, renting, brokering, and auctioning videos all over the world.
- A lifelong activist, David Katz combined his missionary zeal for ecology, his experience working as a foreman and general manager for a large commercial farm, and his passion for organic gardening into a unique consulting practice. He provides information to aspiring and novice organic farmers.

- When David Kalb was phased out of his job in state government, he wanted to help people get through the red tape of dealing with government bureaucracy. So, he applied his previous job experience with his educational background in public administration to create Capital Services, which helps businesses and consumers navigate the complexities of dealing with local, state, and federal government agencies.

- Warren Faidley combined a lifelong fascination for the weather with skills he developed as an amateur photographer and his job experience and contacts as a journalist into a career as a full-time professional weather photographer. He takes photos of hurricanes, storms, tornadoes, and other weather events for newspapers, magazines, and web sites nationwide.

- Theresa Pollack combined the two things she loves most, children and animals, with her passion to help people get over their fear of reptiles. Drawing upon her experience as a preschool teacher and animal trainer and contacts through her husband's reptile store, she provides entertaining educational experiences for children's parties that feature a cadre of exotic snakes, lizards, and other reptiles.

Like all these individuals, once Don focused on what he really wanted, he knew what he needed to do. Since he wanted to stick with architecture, he needed to find a niche for himself in the crowded residential market. After playing with several ideas, he hit upon what he knew would be a winner. Don has a special ability to envision how an existing structure can be transformed to resemble the ideal structure his clients would prefer but can't afford. This crystal talent, coupled with the escalating cost of housing in southern California, led directly to the perfect niche: Don became the architect who could turn an existing home into the owner's dream home. The idea caught on immediately.

How could you combine your passions, experience, background, and contacts with the needs you see around you that people would pay you to help them meet? Make three lists:

1. what you love most

2. your experience, contacts, and background

3. the trends, problems, and unmet needs you notice around you

Then brainstorm possible ways of combining elements of the three lists into various ways you could matrix to find your focus. Be creative. Be imaginative. Play around with the possibilities, even if they seem impractical or silly.

Then, using your inner compass, identify the two or three options that look the brightest and feel the best to you. Start checking them out and trying them on for size. Take your time in finding several scenarios that might fit.

TURBO FUEL: Uncorking Your Creativity

When you're trying to be creative and nothing comes to mind, stop what you're doing and take three deep breaths. Stretch. Shake out the tension in your arms, neck, shoulders, and hands. Get up and walk around, preferably outdoors. Swing your arms, take big strides. Clear your mind by listening to the sounds around you. Can you hear the wind? Are the birds singing? What sounds of life do you hear around you?

If your day is too jam-packed to take even a short break, wait for an idle moment when you would otherwise feel irritated at having to wait, for example, while you're on hold on the telephone, waiting for a slow web site to load, stuck in traffic, or waiting for a fax to come through. When that moment comes, close your eyes, take three deep breaths, and notice what you hear around you.

GET IN STEP: TIMING FOR
A WINNING COMMITMENT

"I'm the best-kept secret in this field," John joked when we first met with him. He was a gifted play therapist, working with severely emotionally disturbed children, but he was spending most of his time doing diagnostic intake interviews at a regional psychiatric center. What he wanted to do was build his small private practice into a full-time niche as a play therapist. That was the purpose of the creative strategy session he scheduled. When John arrived, he talked eagerly about play therapy, the articles he wanted to write, and the research he wanted to do. But whenever we brought the subject around to strategizing how he could build his private practice, he slumped in the chair, glanced down at the floor, and seemed to lose interest.

Brooke did much the same thing when she came for her first strategy session. A baby boomer just by a hair (she was born in 1963), she was a singer with a passion for swing. Her husband was also a musician. They both taught music in the local school district, but they wanted to support themselves by performing together full-time. That's what brought Brooke to us—how to get more bookings and sell lots of the new CD they had planned to make. "There's no interest in Swing right now," she explained, "so we've switched to Pop, and now we're getting a much better response. Our CD will be out next month." The only problem was, she sounded about as excited by all this as if she were talking about an upcoming trip to the dentist for a root canal.

Kyle was pretty bummed out, too. He was a born leader. You could see it in his demeanor, his gait, and his carriage. As he went through the Inner Compass process, he spoke with authority and pride about his role as senior class president and head of his college's student government. After graduating from business school, he was snatched up by a Fortune 500 company and began climbing the ranks of management. But in the past couple of years, he had plateaued. He needed a strategy for getting to the next rung— regional manager—except each time he mentioned ways of getting the position, he would sigh and sink a couple of inches lower in his chair.

Do you think you know what you want to do, too, but, like John, Brooke, and Kyle, do you lose your enthusiasm when it comes to actually planning how you'll do it?

Were these folks off course? Had they turned off their Inner Compass? No, they remained animated and energized whenever they were talking about their goals. They weren't off course, but their timing wasn't right.

John had just gotten married. He and his wife were buying their first home and planning to start a family. While he very much wanted to build a private practice, he didn't want to do it now. His priorities were on having a steady income over the next few years, so he'd have the freedom to concentrate on becoming a husband and father. Once he got clear about that, he could see what he needed to do. Instead of dragging through years doing diagnostic work, which he found dull, and trying to build a private practice, he started looking for a full-time clinical position where he could at least do some play therapy and possibly start a play therapy program. Private practice could come later, after he'd established a reputation and when he could eagerly devote himself to building a clientele.

Truth was, Brooke loved singing and performing, but she didn't like pop music. Her heart was into swing. Although it wasn't popular enough to support her and her husband full-time, swing was about to make a comeback. Looking at their priorities, Brooke and her husband realized they needed to hold tight. Soon, a new generation of listeners would be swinging to the music of Tony Bennett and Frank Sinatra. Meanwhile, they needed to keep their jobs, take as many swing gigs as they could get, build their repertoire and reputation, produce a swing CD, and be ready when the demand came for their unique style.

Kyle was a born leader and he belonged at the helm of a company, but he had just remarried and he and his new wife had two young boys. After work and on weekends, he was busy coaching their soccer team and participating with them in Boy Scout activities. He felt his stepsons needed him at this time, and the regional sales job involved a lot of travel. It wasn't the right position for him at that time in his life. But his career didn't have to plateau. He realized he could seek a more responsible management position within a smaller local company.

TURBO FUEL: A Three-Step Focus Process

Once you get clear about what's most important, it's much easier to know how to focus your time, money, and energy. So, what are your priorities right now? Imagine that you're 100 percent in charge of your future and you could do what you want the way you want. Then use this three-step process to find a focus you can commit to:

1. ASSESS YOUR PRIORITIES

Using this list from *Finding Your Perfect Work,* clarify what matters most to you in life. Feel free to add other priorities to this list. Mark each item as either:

A: essential;   **B: important;**   **C: desirable;**   **N: neutral;**   **U: undesirable**

Keep in mind, now, that we live in a multiple-options era; you can have as many "essential" priorities as is true for you. You may have only one or two "A's" on your list or you may have ten to fifteen, because you won't be happy settling for any fewer.

__ *Acceptance*	__ *Appreciation*	__ *Challenge*	__ *Health*
__ *Admiration*	__ *Quality*	__ *Uniqueness*	__ *Ethics*
__ *Mastery*	__ *Excellence*	__ *Casualness*	__ *Morality*
__ *Creativity*	__ *Originality*	__ *Social and civic*	__ *Surprise*
__ *Comfort*	__ *Informality*	*contribution*	__ *Freedom*
__ *Fitness*	__ *Community*	__ *Variety*	__ *Fame*
__ *Honesty*	*service*	__ *Activity*	__ *Financial*
__ *Spirituality*	__ *Excitement*	__ *Independence*	*security*
__ *Stimulation*	__ *Risk*	__ *Respect*	__ *Fun*
__ *Choice*	__ *Flexibility*	__ *Fortune*	__ *Relaxation*
__ *Prestige*	__ *Recognition*	__ *Prosperity*	__ *Making a lasting*
__ *Stability*	__ *Certainty*	__ *Leisure*	*contribution*
__ *Wealth*	__ *Being well*	__ *Making a*	__ *Peace*
__ *Enjoyment*	*compensated*	*worthwhile*	__ *Personal*
__ *Making a*	__ *Helping and*	*contribution*	*development*
difference	*caring for*	__ *Calm*	__ *Relationships*
__ *Pleasure*	*others*	__ *Wisdom*	__ *Time for your*
__ *Harmony*	__ *Beauty*	__ *Authority*	*partner, lover,*
__ *Growth*	__ *Fulfilling your*	__ *Solitude*	*or spouse*
__ *Power*	*potential*	__ *Being liked*	__ *Time for*
__ *Privacy*	__ *Status*	__ *Accomplishment*	*friends*

__ *Pets*   __ *Popularity*   __ *Competition*   __ *Time for your*

__ *Nature*   __ *Achievement*   __ *Novelty*   *children or*

                                                               grandchildren

2. WEIGH YOUR OPTIONS AND CHOOSE

With your priorities in mind, look back on the two or three matrixing scenarios you have identified, and, if you're not clear which one to choose, try the following process:

- Find a quiet place where you won't be interrupted for at least a half hour.
- Close your eyes and imagine that you're looking at a large blank television screen.
- One by one, project each scenario you're considering onto that screen. Imagine in detail what your life would be like if you committed to taking that particular direction. How would you be using your time? What would your day be like? See the days, weeks, and months ahead of you along that path. How would you feel? What do you like about that scenario? What doesn't feel right? What resistances do you have to it? How could you change it to better fit your values, skills, interests, and desires?
- Once you've viewed each scenario in detail, open your eyes and write in your change journal what you noticed and how you feel about each option. Itemize their pros and cons.
- Then close your eyes again and imagine you're sitting before a bank of several televisions like you would see in a television studio.
- Project all the options you're still considering onto one of those screens, so you can see them side by side before you.
- Compare the various scenarios. Test each one with your inner compass. Which one are you drawn to? Which one do your eyes keeping looking back at? Which one would you most like to be living? Can you combine the best of elements of them into one new scenario?
- Once there's one you clearly prefer, tweak it until you feel excited and enthusiastic about pursuing it.

Here's an example of how this process works. After her second child started school, Jennifer began helping her husband run his pediatric practice. This experience convinced her that she wanted to go back to school so she could pursue her own career working with families. She had been considering three scenarios.

Scenario #1: To go back to school to become a psychologist so she could work in a large research hospital helping to find ways to better assist families of seriously ill children

Scenario #2: To complete her degree as a marriage and family counselor and set up a joint practice with her husband

Scenario #3: To select the best curriculum for creating her own specialty practice, working in transpersonal psychology, and helping families deal with the spiritual aspects of physical and mental health

As she watched these three scenarios unfold, one by one, on a large imaginary screen, she liked all three. She could see each one working well. Her mother had suffered from severe bipolar depression, so Jennifer had always wanted to do something to find better ways to help families cope with this illness. Still, she loved the idea of working side by side with her husband. Spiritual healing was a more recent aspect of her life, and she seemed to have an intuitive sense for it. It was like a special gift. By working with families in this way, she would be pioneering in unexplored territory.

After putting these three scenarios side by side on a bank of TV screens, her preference became clearer. The hospital would be exciting and rewarding. The work with her husband would be fun, but her eye was drawn again and again to the spiritual path. It seemed to draw her in. She felt most at home there. Yes, it also felt most like her inner compass scene in which she was leading a small group of people through the mist over a steep, rocky creek bed. The journey required that she use a large staff to steady her balance. She had selected that staff as the object that represented her inner compass. As she watched the screen playing the spiritual practice scenario, it seemed much like that climb. Yes, that was clearly her choice.

3. MAKE A COMMITMENT

A commitment is a pledge, a promise, a decision to invest yourself in something you're sure you can count on yourself to do. Thus, a commitment is not something to take lightly. Nor should it ever be something you force yourself into. If you don't choose to do something of your own free will, you may not be willing to deliver on your promise and will thus disappoint yourself and anyone else whose life is involved in your decision.

So, as you look at the various scenarios you're considering, are there any you feel willing and eager to commit to? If not, make a sketch of the TV screens you're still considering in your change journal and label each one for future reference. Then make a commitment to gather the information you need either to add to, or alter, what you're considering into one focus you can commit to wholeheartedly with a sense of certainty.

Are You Focused?

- Can you complete this sentence in less than twenty-five words?
  I am committed to . . .

Example:
- completing a master's degree in transpersonal psychology and opening a private practice psychological spiritual counseling
- moving to New Mexico and buying a ranch there where I will lead nature tours
- shifting my business from focusing on computer tutoring to speaking to corporations about the latest technological breakthroughs they should be adopting
- finding a job that will enable me to use my skills as a graphic designer creatively at a salary equal to or above my current position
- retiring in five years with enough income to buy a RV, travel to visit all the national forests, and write a book about my experiences
- Read your focus statement out loud to yourself. How does it sound to you? How do you feel as you read it? Do you believe it? Do you want it to be

true? How strongly do you believe in it? On a scale of 0 to 10, with 0 being "not at all" and 10 being "more than anything in the world," does the focus you're considering committing to score at least a 7 or above? If not, you need to rework your focus until it's more desirable.

- Write your commitment in your change journal. Read it the next morning. Are you still committed? Is it still a 7 or above? Read it at the beginning of next week. Are you still committed? Is it still a 7 or above?

- Read your focus statement to six people and ask them to write down on a slip of paper the one thing they understand you have committed to do. Did they get it? If not, you need to work further on clarifying your focus until people "get it." When they can "get it," you've got it!

- When someone "gets it," ask them how they will know that you've successfully taken your life in that direction, and listen for specific answers that indicate that they understand what you wish to do so well, they'll be able to tell you when:

  - "I'll see your name in the yellow pages offering transpersonal counseling."

  - "I'll get your postcard from New Mexico promoting your nature tours."

  - "You'll be in a new job as a graphic designer, and when you show me a sample of your work, there will be a smile on your face."

  - "I'll be getting an e-mail from you raving about the beauty of one national park after another!"

If those you talk to can't tell you how they'll recognize that you've changed directions, you need to work on making your focus more concrete.

Hung Up? Why We Don't Focus

Thousands of people have attended our workshops on finding your niche, and there has never been a workshop in which we didn't get substantial resistance, at first, to the idea of focusing.

"But, there are so many things I can do. Why limit myself?"

"But, what if I can't make enough money (or find a job) doing that?"

"But what if something better comes along and I miss it?"

"But I don't want to lose out on other opportunities, either."

"But I'm just going to do a little of *this,* so it couldn't hurt to do some of *that,* too."

Do any of these comments sound familiar to you? Are you resisting becoming focused?

We've met people who were so fearful about committing to a focus that they held firmly to the belief they were already focused until everyone else in the group showed them how scattered they appeared to rest of the world. It seems to be a part of human nature to want to wiggle out of focus. And yet, in looking at people who have successfully changed directions to pursue new dreams, the pattern is clear: good luck is when focused effort meets opportunity. This fact became all too painfully clear to Anne, as it does to many.

Anne had been working in customer relations for ten years, but over those years a new dream had begun to grow. She wanted to be a professional speaker, and she had been working on the side toward making that change for several years. She'd been active in Toastmasters and felt at ease on the stage. In fact, she loved being in front of a crowd. She had a bubbly, dynamic, outgoing personality with a knack for making people laugh. But as she sat in our office, describing her plight, disappointment and confusion were written all over her face. Although she always got rave reviews from her audiences, she was getting few bookings.

"I just don't understand it," Anne said, shaking her head and clenching her jaw. "Other people are getting speeches I could do just as well or better!" She often got initial interest to give a presentation, only to have someone else end up with the booking. "What do you speak about?" we asked. "Many things," she responded. "I'm very versatile. I listen to what the organization needs and present an idea for what I could customize just for them. Here's a list of my topics," she offered, reaching into her briefcase and taking out an attractive presentation package. It included a striking black-and-white photo of her in action on the podium and a tastefully laid-out sheet of stationery, listing twenty-five different topics she could speak about.

This list held the clue to Anne's problem. "Tell us about the last speech you lost to someone else," we posed. She described a scenario that had become a pattern. A company needed a speech on leadership for a management meeting. They had gotten her name as a referral from someone who had heard her speak on a related topic. She listened to what they wanted and submitted a description, outline, and price for her presentation. When she called to see if her materials had arrived, her contact confirmed that they had received it and expressed satisfaction with what she'd sent. But, after not hearing back from them, Anne called again, only to learn that someone else had been hired for the job.

"Who did they hire?" we wanted to know. "Another speaker," Anne answered. "But who?" we repeated. As we pressed for details, she realized the pattern, herself. The speaker that the company hired had written a book on leadership. The speaker that another company hired to address the subject of corporate etiquette conducted executive workshops nationwide on that topic. Another person who had been selected over Anne had spoken exclusively on the topic at hand for many years.

Anne was losing business to speaker after speaker who had focused on one field of expertise that they had become known as experts in. "But I couldn't do that!" she grimaced. "I'd never get any work if I only spoke on one topic! Anyway, it would get boring." Yet that's what her competition was doing, and they were getting the business. Reluctantly, Anne began working to identify a focus for herself. She settled on customer service. She had ample experience and credibility in this field upon which to draw, she especially enjoyed talking to colleagues, and there was certainly a demand for the topic. Once Anne had a focus for her programs, her bookings grew and she was on her way to a new future. Surprisingly, once people knew of her specialty, she was also asked to speak to customer-service personnel on a wider range of topics.

So, while there are many excuses people give for not wanting to focus, the underlying causes are often less obvious.

INDECISION: WORRYING ALL OVER THE PLACE

Anne had clearly been afraid to commit to any given focus. She wanted to be the speaker for all occasions; as a result, she was hired for few. She was worried that she would be bored. She was worried there wouldn't be enough opportunities in her own niche. She was worried she would lose out to others if she focused her topics. But her fears were based on erroneous conclusions. Instead of limiting her success, focusing was enhancing it.

What are you afraid will happen if you commit to a specific focus for your future? What evidence do you have that that's what would happen? What erroneous conclusions could you be operating on? How could you check out whether your fear is realistic?

CONFUSION: AFRAID TO CONFRONT CHOICES

Selecting one clear and specific direction for our future involves making decisions. But once we make a decision, we're only a step away from action. As long as we remain vague, confused, and unclear about what we want to do, we won't have to decide, and then we won't have to take action. Think for a moment about Dorothea, the woman who had recently retired and taken on too many projects for other people to have time for achieving her goal of illustrating children's books. As long as Dorothea remained confused about why she wasn't enjoying her newfound freedom, she wouldn't have to choose between her own interests and those of her husband and daughter.

Once Dorothea saw what was happening, though, she had to take a stand. Define herself. Identify priorities. Draw boundaries. Set limits. How much time could she spend helping her husband and still have time for her own projects? How much time could she devote to caring for her grandchildren without detracting from enjoying long-awaited time with her husband? These were tough choices. But once she made them, she would be able to set up a schedule that took into account everyone's needs, including hers.

She decided to explain to her daughter she couldn't take care of the babies during the week, but she would gladly serve as backup in the case of emergencies . . . as long as there weren't too many. She talked with her husband about hiring a service to do the bookkeeping so they could spend more leisure time together. To her surprise, her husband was delighted. Golfing with her in the afternoon was more fun for him than having her in his office, hovering over the computer.

Are you faced with having to make choices you're afraid to confront? Who might you displease or disappoint? What would happen if you clarified your intentions and talked them out with those involved?

TURBO FUEL: Walk Away Doubt

When you're feeling confused, take a long walk to clear your mind, preferably in a park or other natural setting. When you return, focus your attention on what you do know. Write it down or talk it out: "What I do know is . . ." Before you know it, you'll be clear on what you do and don't want and what you need to do about it.

VACILLATION: SENDING UP TRIAL BALLOONS

"Today I'm sure X is the best direction I could go. Tomorrow, I won't give a hoot about X because I'll be all excited about Y . . . until the next day when I'll be on to Z." Such vacillation isn't an unusual experience when changing directions, even when we're tuned into our inner compass. But it is a frustrating one. "I just want to settle on something and get it over with," Marshal told us, having decided to leave the practice of law. "My mother is the one who wanted me to be a lawyer. I was preparing for it ever since I was a kid. I've never thought about doing anything else until now. It's like getting the opportunity to date every good-looking woman you meet!"

Like Marshal, when we've said goodbye to the situation we've been in up to this point in our lives, unless we already know where we want to go, it's like opening Pandora's Box. One day, we might be thinking about doing something real practical, like our father might recommend. The next day, we're off in the clouds, dreaming about our wildest fantasies. This type of vacillation is only natural. It's somewhat like how Gloria had to try out lots of new experiences before she could discover what she liked about her job. We may need to try out or audition various scenarios for our life before we can settle on one. That's okay.

Unless idea-hopping becomes a chronic situation, many of us need time to synthesize or refine our feelings and digest what we're discovering about the feasibility of our ideas before we can know that we've found the right one. That's the only way we'll find what we truly want. It's like selecting a wedding dress. You really don't want to buy the first one you try on. You want to find that perfect one.

Give yourself the time and permission to send up some trial balloons and find out what the weather is like out there.

Of course, sometimes the pressure of change doesn't give us the luxury of finding the perfect direction. Sometimes, we have to act quickly. If this is your situation and you must act now, choose your best available option as a "interim" focus from which to explore further, as Vicki did. Having left the field of journalism after twenty-two years, she wanted to explore creating a small business-oriented web site, doing a series of small business seminars or offering small business consulting services. The problem was she needed time to explore the feasibility of these possibilities. She needed an interim strategy that would both support her through the transition and give her time to test the waters for the ideal platform for her business. Her solution was to take on a project working with a small start-up Internet company.

This strategy gave her the opportunity to continue focusing on her ultimate goal. "The only challenge," she warned, to this otherwise ideal solution, "is that I have to keep telling them I don't want to take another full-time job, and they keep making more and more appealing offers." But she remains focused on enjoying her independence.

Once you have a focus, you know where you're going. All you have to do next is figure out how you'll get there.

Breakthrough: Joann

Joann had worked for fifteen years as an attorney before she got Hodgkin's disease. She never enjoyed the practice of law, so the illness provided an opportunity for her to question what she wanted to do with her life, and, frankly, she didn't know. But she had an ingenious idea for how to find out. She sent letters to people who knew her, asking them what career they thought would best suit her. As a result, she obtained her Ph.D. in child development and now works as a resident psychologist at the New York Foundling Hospital in New York City, an establishment that cares for very sick and/or severely disabled children.

Some of the children are in the hospital for rehabilitative purposes, but many are there for long periods, some for their entire short life spans. Joann has worked there with these children for four years now and has many heartwarming stories to share. She has never been happier.

CLOSING REFLECTION

Is there a clear focus you're ready to make a commitment to? Yes or no? What are you willing to commit to doing at this point? This is your journey. You need not be any further along than where you are.

> *You see things and say, "why?" but I dream things that never were and say, "why not?"*
> — GEORGE BERNARD SHAW

DISCOVERING HOW TO GET THERE FROM HERE: DEVELOPING A STRATEGY

What you do to get somewhere is who you become when you arrive.

—GENEEN ROTH

Hello," the airline ticket agent answered, greeting yet another caller wanting to book a reservation. "Where are you wanting to go?" was, of course, her first question. The caller presented his dilemma. He had to get from Santa Barbara, California, to Waterloo, Iowa, for a meeting at 9:00 A.M. two weeks from Friday. The agent proceeded to present various itineraries for the caller to choose from. Some took him through Los Angeles and Minneapolis; others, through Phoenix and Minneapolis; and still others, through Los Angeles and St. Louis.

- If he was willing to leave on Wednesday and arrive on Thursday morning before Friday's meeting, he could get there for only $414.

111

- For $869, he could leave mid-morning Thursday and arrive past 11:00 P.M. the night before the meeting.
- Another route, at only $453 round trip, would require him to leave Santa Barbara at 5:45 A.M. and arrive in Waterloo mid-afternoon the day before the meeting.
- For just under $500, he could leave at 7:45 A.M. and arrive at 10:00 P.M. Thursday, but there would be a three-hour layover in L.A. and a two-hour layover in St. Louis.

The traveler considered his situation and weighed the alternatives. Time was a key factor. He wanted to spend as little time traveling as possible, but he also wanted to leave as late on Thursday morning as possible and get there as early as possible Thursday evening. Money, of course, was another key factor. He wanted to spend as little as possible, yet comfort was also important. He didn't want to sit through hours of layovers. Given these criteria, he opted for the $500 route, figuring the saner arrival and departure times would leave him more rested for the meeting, despite longer layovers. The agent made the reservations immediately, and soon the traveler had a printed itinerary for his trip.

This brief interaction illustrates the elements involved in developing a strategy and how straightforward it can be when you know where you are, where you want to go, and the criteria you have for getting there. If only changing directions could be that easy! Actually, it can. It was for Marcus. He had practiced podiatry for ten years before managed care began cutting deeply into his income. As he watched his bank balance declining and his cost of doing business increasing, he started considering other alternatives. If he wanted to avoid bankruptcy, he had to make a change and he had to do it rapidly.

Marcus wanted to stay in the health care field, continue to be self-employed, earn at least $60,000 a year, and cut down on the pressure of having a high-overhead office. So he began considering a variety of health-related fields, including nursing, physical therapy, medical billing, and medical transcription. Nursing didn't offer many opportunities to be self-employed. Physical therapy would require that he return to school for a considerable period of time. In his community, there seemed to be a glut of people offering medical billing, so after reviewing his options he decided to pursue a new career in medical transcription.

Given his situation, Marcus began looking for the quickest way to shift into his new career. He was familiar with most medical terms and knew many health care practitioners, but after taking a sample proficiency test on the Web, he didn't feel ready to start without some additional training. He discovered several training programs through vocational schools and community colleges. But those took quite some time to complete. Instead, he decided upon an accredited home-study course he could complete within just a few months by working at his own pace during evenings and weekends. An added feature of this program was that, upon graduation, it also provided referrals to practitioners needing transcription services.

So, soon Marcus had a strategy—an itinerary for getting from where he was to where he needed to be before his money ran out and he went in the hole.

1. He would keep his podiatry practice going until he completed his course of study.
2. Meanwhile, he would set up a home office, purchase medical billing software, prepare new business cards, stationery and marketing materials, and begin plans to close his practice when his lease ran out in eight months.
3. Upon completing his home-study course, he would take some referrals from the training company to get started but would also begin immediately to solicit other clients through his own contacts with hospitals, clinics, and private physicians' offices, contact transcription services that contract out to freelancers, and solicit overload from other transcriptionists.

This clear-cut strategy worked for Marcus. But finding a strategy isn't always so clear-cut. In fact, developing a strategy is the best way we've found for testing whether you've actually committed unequivocally to a specific focus. If you haven't, if you've just fooled yourself into thinking you're focused, you won't be able to develop a strategy.

Just imagine how the opening conversation with the airline ticket agent would have gone if the traveler on the phone couldn't decide whether he wanted to go to Waterloo or Des Moines.

Without a clear destination, finding a strategy might go more like it did for Bob. He came to one of our retreats, so eager to start working on his strategy that he resisted going through the first day's clarifying process. "Can't I just skip this?" he wanted to know. "Couldn't we just get right to the bottom line and lay out a strategy?" Once we convinced him to follow the agenda, he was startled to discover he couldn't describe the new company he wanted to start in a way that any of us could understand what it was he would be offering. "Well, it will be on the Internet," he explained. "But it will also be a physical center where companies can bring their personnel. It draws on my extensive background as a sales trainer with the company I've been with, but I'll pull in the expertise and resources of many other experts as well. It will be a place where sales personnel can support one another. And I'll be traveling a lot and writing on sales training, too."

"Oh," one of the participants offered, "you'll be a sales trainer, then." "No, not exactly," Bob responded. "Much more than that."

"Oh, I get it," someone else offered. "You'll be creating a master sales training site on the Internet, with online courses." "Well, I'll do some of that, but that's only a part of it," Bob replied.

"You're going to create a sales training center and promote it on the Internet?" someone else posed, looking puzzled. "Well, that too," Bob explained.

"So," we asked, hoping to draw his intention out further, "what do you see as your first step?" "That's what I'm here for," Bob responded in frustration. "I need a strategy and I don't know where to start."

Bob had pulled together a smattering of all the things he enjoyed and wanted to do, but these ideas were not yet a destination. They were more like a collection of possibilities. Before he could develop a strategy, he needed to hone down or combine some of the things he was interested in into a specific intention. So we took him through the Choosing a Focus Process (described in chapter four). He was able to project four scenarios onto his imaginary bank of TV screens:

1. Working as a sales trainer traveling all over the world
2. Creating and running a pre-eminent, interactive web site for sales personnel
3. Operating a sales training center staffed by other trainers with many ongoing support group functions for independent salespeople
4. Writing books and articles on sales training

As Bob considered these options, he synthesized them into a clear direction: he wanted to become one of the world's top independent sales trainers and spend most his time traveling to corporate training events. To enable those he had trained to keep in touch with him and continue as his clients, he would provide an interactive web site where they could get ongoing support and expertise from him and other related experts. Full access to his web site would be reserved for those who had participated in his training programs, and he would contribute regular articles to the site to enhance its value.

With such a clearly stated intention or destination, we could assist Bob in developing a strategy as follows:

1. Pull together his expertise into a series of training courses
2. Test and refine the courses and gather references and testimonials from satisfied participants
3. Develop a plan and accompanying materials for marketing the sales training courses
4. Write articles for trade magazines based on the material in his courses to draw attention to himself as an expert
5. Build a web site where interested clients and participants from his training programs could obtain further information. Begin by turning the articles he's been writing into an online and e-mail newsletter

6. Recruit other experts to participate on the web site as content providers and, in the process, build connections with them as important referral sources for corporate training opportunities

Eight out of ten people seeking to develop a strategy discover they have to go back to Stage Four and refine their intention. How about you? Can you complete the following sentence in ten or fewer words? I need to know how I can . . . (fill in your intention)

For example:

I need to know how I can:

- *Create an e-commerce web site.*
- *Become a fiction writer.*
- *Get a job on a cruise ship.*
- *Start a business as a professional organizer.*

If so, you have a simply stated intention; you're ready to strategize. If not, go back through Committing to a Focus on pages 90–103 in chapter four.

The Task: Charting a Course—
The C's & R's of Creative Change

A strategy, like a travel itinerary, is a series of specific steps we can take to get from where we are to where we want to be. It's a plan for how to marshal all the resources available within our existing situation, whatever they might be, to accomplish a particular goal or result. In other words, a strategy is how we'll use our time, our money, and our energy to make the changes we want to make. Actually, we're always operating with a strategy, but often it's a de facto one, meaning, we're doing it without knowing what we're doing.

If you recall, Ben had been laid off from his job as a textbook editor. The de facto strategy he'd used all his life had been "something will come along." That strategy had worked out fine up until this point in his life, so he'd never really questioned or even noticed that it was his strategy for getting ahead in life. But this de facto strategy wasn't working anymore. He was questioning whether there was more to life than whatever came along. He wanted to take writers to northern Italy and lead creative writing workshops there, but he couldn't see how that could ever happen, because, if he relied on his familiar de facto strategy, it wouldn't.

Nothing was going to come along to take Ben to Italy to do writing workshops. To do that, he would have to make something happen, and that would require a new strategy. De facto strategies are reactive in nature. They put us in the position of responding to what's happening to us, instead of enabling us to orchestrate what will happen. So, with de facto strategies, we get trapped in the Someday Syndrome—wishing and hoping that "someday, my dream will come" but wondering why it never does.

Are you relying on a de facto strategy to change your life? Something like "I don't know what to do, so I'll just wait and see." Or, "I'm confused, so all I can do is just hope for the best." Or, "Surely something will come along, if I just keep doing a good job at what I'm doing." Or, "If I keep going, maybe I'll fall into something better." Or, "Someday I'll get a break." Or, if all else fails, "Maybe I'll win the lottery." Have you adopted someone else's strategy, doing what they think you should do because it worked for them, instead of what would work for you?

Since de facto strategies usually don't work very well, we don't like to admit that we rely on them. But unless we consciously select an alternative strategy, we will end up depending on a de facto one. In other words, unless otherwise specified, our favorite de facto strategy will kick in. To chart a course to where we want to go, we have to consciously create a strategy that works for us, our situation, and our particular destination. This requires (1) knowing what you're up for, your "change style," so to speak, (2) getting clear about your situation, (3) being creative about options, and (4) deciding what you'll actually commit to doing.

We call these requirements the four C's of Creative Change.

COMFORT: What's Your Style?
CLARITY: What's Your Situation?
CREATIVITY: What Are Your Options?

COMMITMENT: What Have You Done So Far? What Will You Do Next?

As Gregg, a New York clothing designer, discovered, meeting these requirements usually demands that he do something different from what he's been doing. Gregg's career as an independent designer was sailing high. And he loved his work . . . until his high-fashion world turned upside down. A rash of department stores closed. Grunge replaced elegance. Jeans and jogging suits with sneakers became the haute couture of the day.

Gregg panicked. He tried one strategy after another to restore interest in his upscale designs. He crisscrossed the country, doing trunk showings in small retail stores. He held fashion shows at upscale restaurants. He created a line of polyester print dresses. He even moved his operations to Los Angeles and opened a showroom there, but the L.A. economy soon hit a slump even worse than New York's. "Will this ever be fun again?" he wondered, as he kept plunging ahead. The answer seemed to be "no," until finally, Gregg put a stop to everything. He flew to New York and welcomed the New Year in at an ashram in the Catskills.

This week away enabled Gregg to return to Los Angeles feeling renewed and refreshed. It was as if someone had changed the prescription of his eyeglasses. He saw his life in a new light. First, he stopped representing clients who were nothing but headaches. He sought out a partner who enjoyed handling the aspects of the business he found most unpleasant, leaving him with the time to cultivate new clients and develop foreign markets for his designs. Instead of his morning latté, he began meditating each morning and tending his garden. He also began taking time to nurture a renewed interest in playing polo. His head began to clear, and he could see a new direction for the future of his business. The problems that had been driving him crazy no longer bothered him. He was running his business instead of letting it run him.

As Gregg found, to develop an effective strategy, we usually need to step away from the demands and responsibilities of our current situation so we can rest, relax, and reflect creatively on each of these issues. We call these requirements the four R's of Creative Change:

RETREAT: step outside of the parameters and limitations of your current situation.

REST: build up your energy so we can be enthusiastic about developing a new strategy. It's hard to be both clear and creative in a low state of energy.

RELAX: connect with your inner compass so you can get into a creativity state of mind.

REFLECT: so you can see clearly where you've been, where you are, and where you want to go.

TURBO FUEL: A Creative Space

Find a creative space where you can rest, relax, and recharge. It could be a spa, a vacation resort, a retreat, or an ashram such as Gregg found. Or it might be a special room in your home, a nook in your garden, or a favorite nearby spot in nature like a lakeshore, a forest, the seaside, or a desert. It might be the sanctuary of a church or even a secluded bench in a quiet city park.

Research at the University of Michigan shows that viewing beautiful surroundings focuses attention, helps us make better plans, and deflects distractions while lowing irritability. People handle things better and get more done without getting overwhelmed when they get away to scenic locales. So arrange to get away from your current responsibilities to reflect quietly on the questions that lie at the heart of the four C's of creative change.

Comfort: What's Your Style?
What Are You Up For?

Some people are parachutists at heart; they love to leap into the unknowns of their future and land on their feet. Others are more like tight-wire artists; they like to make their way carefully, step-by-step, across the gulf between today's realities and tomorrow's dreams. Still others are more like trapeze artists; they'd rather have a helping hand to catch and carry them into their future. These preferences reflect three broad-brush approaches that we usually have to choose among for developing a strategy, as we plan for getting where we want to go. Each has its pros and cons.

TAKING A FLYING LEAP

To Mike's friends and family, it looked as if he were about to head down a risky and dangerous road. But, like a parachutist who has carefully packed his chute, Mike was well prepared to step into a new future. He had been working for an instructional design firm, and the clients he served were quite pleased with his work. "You are the best!" they kept telling him, when he turned over his finished product. "You ought to go out on your own. We'd be your first client!"

This continual stream of praise and encouragement got Mike to thinking. His employer was billing clients nine times his hourly rate. If he went out on his own, he could charge his own clients considerably less and increase his income. Excluding office meetings and office politics, Mike calculated his actual work was only taking him five hours a day.

Soon, he had a clear-cut goal: create his own instructional design firm. But he wasn't interested in starting his venture on the side. He didn't want to ease gradually into his business. First, it could create a conflict of interest with his employer. Second, he wanted to make a clean break. So he laid out a strategy like a carefully packed parachute:

1. Set up and select a name for his organization as a legal entity
2. Calculate his start-up and operating costs and set his prices
3. Create business cards and marketing materials
4. Make contacts with key referral sources
5. Give two-week's notice to his employer
6. Line up his first client during those two weeks
7. Take the leap

Mike had a client starting on Day One of his new life. Was it a risky thing to do? Well, it would be for many people, but not for Mike. He was ideally positioned to leap straight from his old life to his new one. He already had an excellent reputation in his field and a client base to start out with. The finances added up in his favor. And, best of all, he was able to make three times the money working only five hours a day!

Are you and your situation well suited to take a leap straight into your future, or do you need to ease your way more gradually into a new life?

Flying Leap: Moving Directly from the Old to the New Life:
All Planning Done Beforehand

PROS	CONS
■ *Chance for total commitment*	■ *Little leeway for mistakes*
■ *No waiting around*	■ *No opportunity to learn as you go*
■ *Can be 100% focused*	■ *Do-or-die pressure*
■ *No confusion for others about what you're doing*	■ *No security if you change your mind or adjust course as you go*

STEPPING STONES

As Ben started to contemplate the possibility of actually doing creative-writing retreats in northern Italy, there was no way he could leap directly into supporting himself from where he was at the moment. It was out of the question. Although he spoke Italian fluently and knew northern Italy well, he had never conducted a writers' workshop. Although he had many ideas, he had no curriculum prepared. Although he knew many writers, he had no idea if they would pay for a weeklong retreat in a foreign country. And to bring in the income he needed to contribute to the family and cover his costs of putting on the workshop, he would need no fewer than three workshops a year consisting of thirty writers per workshop, paying at least $1,800 plus their travel expenses. How could he attract that many writers to commit to that level of time and money with an unknown workshop leader?

Clearly, Ben needed to develop a strategy that would provide a series of stepping stones from which he could discover the feasibility of his idea and move, step-by-step, from life as an editor to life as a leader of exotic writers' retreats. There were far too many unknown variables to plan this whole shift in lifestyle beforehand. Although he knew he'd like teaching retreats in Italy, he wasn't at all sure he was up to recruiting ninety writers each year to attend them.

So Ben developed what we call a Stepping Stone Strategy:

1. He would actively seek out a full-time, 9-to-5 editorial position. He chose this option over freelance work so he would have a guaranteed income base, with evenings and weekends free to explore creating a new life without the pressures of lining up clients.

2. He would begin developing a creative writers' workshop and start testing out its value by offering it as a low-cost, local adult-education program. Since the sponsoring organization markets such programs, Ben wouldn't have to deal with enrolling writers himself until he knew what would draw them and had the reputation and experience to make recruitment easier.

3. He would research other writers' retreats and attend some himself.

4. Once he began attracting a following of writers, he would test out sponsoring a weekend retreat in a nearby resort community. This would allow him to discover if writers would pay for a getaway retreat with him.

5. Then, if his local writers' retreats became successful, he would experiment with scheduling one of the retreats to northern Italy. Ben calculated that he would need at least three years to get to this point in the process, and planned to offer his first Italian retreat by the end of those two years.

6. Once he discovered he could fill one retreat a year for a couple of years, he would consider leaving his job.

Of course, not all stepping-stone strategies take as long as Ben's, but this approach does involve taking one step and planning the next one, based upon the experience and results of the previous ones. Stepping-stones strategies usually including taking a variety of interim steps, such as keeping a job you're hoping to leave while studying to enter a new field or while preparing, as Ben was, for a new endeavor. Other stepping stones might include doing temp work, freelancing, volunteering, or interning under someone, taking a sabbatical, living off savings, and cutting back living expenses to rely on a spouse's income while going back to school, and so forth.

Are your nature and your situation better suited to a more gradual stepping-stone approach to the future?

Stepping Stones: Moving Gradually, One Step at a Time, into a New Life: Planning Is Done at Each Step Along the Way

PROS	CONS
▪ *Safer, more gradual approach*	▪ *Change occurs slowly*
▪ *You can always go back*	▪ *You may miss a window of opportunity*
▪ *Better options may appear*	▪ *You can't devote 100% of your energy*
▪ *You can learn as you go and*	*to the new goal*
adjust your plans, based on what	▪ *Your focus is split between old and new:*
you discover along the way	*this can be distracting and exhaust-*
	ing and possibly confusing to others

A HELPING HAND

Martha was a nurse practitioner working in a family shelter when she realized that many homeless women were not getting prenatal care, and no other community organization planned to fill this need. She decided she would. That decision changed the course of her life. She didn't have the means to underwrite such a venture herself, so she took a grant-writing class and wrote a grant proposal. The resulting $52,000 grant from a San Francisco foundation enabled her to launch the San Francisco Prenatal Care Program, a nonprofit organization providing medical care for homeless pregnant women. The foundation grant was her helping hand. Even with the grant, the first two years of getting the program under way were difficult. Martha was doing everything herself, while working part-time. Additional grants and fund-raising efforts, however, helped the clinic grow to a staff of sixteen. Martha now serves as executive director and fund-raiser, and limits her work outside the clinic to only one day a week.

Diane also needed a helping hand to change the course of her life, but hers came through an entirely different route. As a teenager, she had dreamed of becoming an artist, but she married one instead and settled into a life as a wife and mother. When divorce left her with no income, through the suggestion of a friend she contacted her state's department of vocational rehabilitation. They offered a variety of grants to assist disabled individuals, including displaced homemakers, to re-enter the workforce. Diane presented them with her idea of creating a center for feminine arts, which would include self-discovery and creative-expression workshops.

Skeptical at first, the state representative attended a workshop Diane conducted at a community college, and from that point on they knew she was serious about her plans to become a commercial fine artist and art educator. The agency sent her to five small business administration seminars on starting a business, which she attended over three months. They also required that she write a business plan. Using the knowledge gained in the seminars and working eighteen hours a day for over thirty days, she developed and submitted a plan requesting $35,000 in funds for equipment and initial materials. After a few months of red tape, a lot of patience and determination, and investing every financial asset of her own, including a $22,000 home equity loan, the grant was approved, and Diane had the helping hand she needed to take her life in a new direction.

A helping hand can be a loan, a grant, or simply the opportunity to move back into your parents' home while you redirect your life. It can be assistance from a mentor who decides to help promote the efforts of an aspiring colleague. Or it can be a family member who offers to pave the way for a loved one by opening doors to key contacts. But as Martha's and Diane's stories illustrate, a helping hand is usually no easy ride. Sometimes, as in both their cases, this strategy requires extensive preparation and planning to convince those involved that a proposed strategy will be viable. And, usually, there will be performance standards and requirements to meet.

Unless it's from a loving relative or friend, getting a helping hand requires that we have something in mind that others consider to be significant enough to invest in. As Martha points out, "There has to be a need for what you're asking money for. You have to show that you can fulfill that need and how you will evaluate the success of your work, because people want to support successes." This means, as Diane found, "You have to believe in yourself and develop a lot of self-discipline."

Martha's strategy began with searching through the foundation and grant libraries in her city. She looked for foundations that funded the kind of projects she had in mind. Then, she wrote a letter of intent indicating:

1. What she wanted to do
2. How much money she needed
3. What the project would do
4. How she was going to evaluate it

Foundations that were interested responded by asking her to submit a full proposal, and, since each foundation had its own guidelines and expectations, she had to tailor a separate proposal to each funding source. Then came the next hurdle: mastering the art of rejection and marshaling the persistence to continue her search until she found her helping hand.

Sources of Financial Help

▪ *Loans from family and friends:* This is the most common way people finance new dreams. To establish an appropriate interest rate when borrowing from friends and family, visit the St. Louis Central Reserve Bank's web site, www.stls.frb.org,where you'll find rates you can use as a reference.

▪ *Personal loans or lines of credit:* If you or your spouse have an existing job and a good credit record, some banks will make personal loans or offer a line of credit, as will credit unions. To check out loans you might qualify for, visit Quicken's Cash Finder Program at www.cashfinder.com.

- *Home equity loans:* If you own your home, you may be able to refinance your home loan and use the funds as a reservoir for undertaking a new direction.

- *Character-based microloans:* The Small Business Administration (SBA) and private foundations grant very small loans (from under $100 to $25,000) to eligible individuals starting small businesses, based on the quality of the idea and the individual's ability to carry it out. See the SBA web site, www.sba.online.sba.gov, for programs near you, or call (800) 8-ASK-SBA.

- *Grants or scholarships:* For more information on obtaining a grant, see books like *The Complete Guide to Getting a Grant* by Laurie Blum (Wiley), *Selling Goodness* by Michael Levine (Renaissance Media), *I'll Grant You That* by Jim Burke and Carol Ann Prater (Heinemann), and *Grantseeker's Toolkit* by Cheryl Carter New and James Aaron Quick (John Wiley & Sons).

- *Investors:* The best investors are people in your local area or others who know you personally and/or are highly involved, experienced, and/or interested in the nature of your new direction. For more on finding investors, visit www.americanexpress.com, quicken.com/banking_and_credit, and www.venturea.com.&-articles.

A microloan from the Working Capital lending group was Cynthia's helping hand. For several years, she had been trying to grow her part-time business, taking people on dogsled tours in the New Hampshire mountains. But she needed new harnesses, gang lines, and other equipment, and she needed money to do advertising. By joining the Working Capital lending group, Cynthia was able to get a microloan to cover these expenses. They didn't ask about her credit history, but they did want to know about her business, why they should give the loan, and what she would do to repay it.

She had no problem repaying the loan, however, because the marketing efforts it financed attracted a sizable contract with a local ski area.

Of course, as we mentioned, a helping hand doesn't always involve financial assistance. For Barrie, it was an offer of free space by a mentor, where she could conduct her first career transition seminars. For Denise, it was the opportunity to live with her parents while she healed from the debilitating illness that caused her to seek a new career and a new life. For Rick, it was his father's printing Rick's T-shirt designs at cost on his printing press. For Linda, it was donations of furniture, draperies, silverware, and decorating talent for her new bed-and-breakfast inn. Without the outpouring of such community support Linda wouldn't have be able to create her dream to open the first B&B in the small mountain village where she lives.

Are your nature and your situation such that getting a helping hand would be the best strategy for launching your future? What type of assistance do you need? What are your most likely sources of help?

Helping Hand: Finding Others to Ease the Way
Planning Must Convince Others to Invest

PROS	CONS
▪ *Reduces the risk of changing directions*	▪ *Others are counting on you: you have moral and perhaps legal obligations*
▪ *Provides a base to grow from*	▪ *Often involves lots of paperwork and reporting*
▪ *Sometimes not otherwise possible*	
▪ *Prevents undercapitalization*	▪ *Can lead to overdependence on others*
▪ *You're not alone; you have the support and backing of others*	▪ *You may be encumbered by a debt load*
	▪ *Your helping hand may become a meddling hand*

Sometimes, it's possible to combine aspects of these three change styles: flying leap, stepping stones, and helping hand. That was the case for Linda in starting her B&B. In addition to a helping hand from the community, she had some important stepping stones to rely on. She had run a day spa in her village for two years, so she would rely on income from the day spa to support herself while she got the B&B going. Also, her spa clients became some of her first clients and served as great referral sources.

Clarity: What's the Situation?

Had the traveler who wanted to get from Santa Barbara to Waterloo been wanting to fly from Los Angeles to New York City, finding an itinerary to meet his needs would have been much simpler. But his situation made finding a suitable route more challenging. And so it is with developing a strategy to change our lives; our situation contributes to just how complex or simple the change we want will be.

Mike, if you recall, was ideally positioned to make the transition to his own instructional design company. He was well known and had extensive experience in his field. He had a number of potential clients eager to work with him because not only was he good at what he did, but he could save them a lot of money. His situation made changing directions easier. But Valerie's situation was quite different.

If you recall, Valerie was working as an administrative assistant when she acquired a disease that led her to develop a passion for fitness, and she wanted to devote her life to teaching people about how exercise, posture, nutrition, movement, and breathing could prevent or correct work-related injuries. She had identified her niche, but with little experience other than her own positive results from working out at the gym, if she was going to change directions she would have to take a good look at her situation and develop a strategy to overcome this limitation. To check out her situation, she consulted numerous fitness and heath experts, and ascertained the following:

Although Valerie had developed her own methods, via trial and error, that worked well for her, she realized that pursuing her niche of combining fitness and ergonomics would require a higher level of knowledge than she possessed. She would need to take some basic exercise science courses like anatomy, exercise physiology, biomechanics, and kinesiology and to obtain CPR (cardiopulmonary resuscitation) certification. If she obtained an advanced degree in a related field, she would have still better opportunities to pursue her new career. Or she could garner the needed credentials more quickly by obtaining certification from one or more of the nationally recognized organizations in the field.

Because there are many fitness and bodywork modalities, Valerie also realized she would need to explore a variety of approaches and decide if she wanted to specialize in one or more of them or stick with her own unique approach. Either way, she would need to be able to explain how what she does is both similar to and different from the approaches other people are using. She also discovered that if she wanted to earn more than about $20,000 to $25,000 a year, she would need to establish herself as a high-profile independent consultant with corporate clients, instead of working as an employee within an organization or working one-on-one with individual clients.

Facing her situation was daunting, but it didn't extinguish Valerie's desire. Instead, knowing where she stood, she chose to develop a stepping-stone strategy. She would keep her job, begin taking some basic fitness-related classes, and reflect further on her options as she learned more about the field.

Your strategy can never be any better than your understanding of your situation. What is your situation? What are your strengths? In what ways are you well positioned and prepared to proceed in the direction of your new focus? What are your weaknesses? In what ways are you poorly positioned and unprepared to head in your desired direction?

Assessing Your Situation

1. What skills, abilities, resources, equipment, or contacts are required to move in the direction you're considering?
2. Which of these do you already possess? Which must you acquire?
3. What's in your treasure chest? What advantages do you have? What do you bring to the situation that would predispose you

to success, i.e., credentials, capability, credibility, connections?

4. In what ways are you at a disadvantage?

5. How easy is it for people to move in the direction you're seeking? What seems to make the difference between those who have done it successfully and those who have tried but not succeeded?

6. What difficulties are most often associated with moving in this direction? How can you surmount them?

7. How is what you're seeking to do customarily done? Can you do it this way, or will you need to find an unaccustomed, alternative route?

8. What is the typical time frame for accomplishing the new direction you wish to undertake? Do you have the time required before you must make a change? How can you arrange your life to take the time required?

9. What are the costs involved in your making this change? What is your financial situation? How can you finance this change?

10. What about your current situation will be an asset in moving in your new direction? What will be a hindrance?

11. Can what you're seeking to do be started while maintaining your current situation, or will you need to make a clean break or find some interim solution while you change directions?

Creativity: What Are Your Options?

Since graduating from college, Carlos had been working as a graphic designer in a corporate art department. He liked the work, but it was starting to feel monotonous. He wanted to do something more creative that involved his two favorite activities: travel and photography. In working with his inner compass and matrixing his interests, abilities, and skills, he settled on the goal of becoming a travel photographer, working perhaps for a travel magazine, either freelance or on salary. But he realized that, given his situation, this would be no easy or overnight feat.

He learned that travel photography was a difficult field to break into, with most of the well-paying magazines using only experienced professionals. With no job experience in either field, he couldn't just log on to some job web sites or check out the want ads and land a job. Also, travel photographers may work long hours for many years before they can earn what Carlos had become accustomed to. On the plus side, though, he had worked with photographers through the art department and had some contacts. He already owned top-notch camera equipment, knew how to use various computer programs for integrating photos and text, and didn't mind working long hours, especially if he was traveling. In addition, he was young, single, and ready to change. But he needed a strategy.

After reading a stack of books, surfing dozens of web sites, and talking with a variety of people associated with the world of travel magazines, he generated a number of possible strategies, each of which would involve taking a stepping-stone approach for getting from graphic designer to travel photographer.

1. He could seek a job in the art department of a travel magazine and work his way laterally into the photography side of the business.

2. He could keep his current job and enroll in an evening college-level photography program and take photographic workshops and photo tours where magazine editors sometimes scout out new talent.

3. He could apprentice himself on the side to one of the photographers he knew, in hopes of parlaying the experience into an opportunity to take assignments his mentor didn't have the time or desire to take on.

4. He could take a more direct approach and start developing his own style of work, building a photo portfolio and sending it on spec to smaller publications. Once he had a track record, he could parlay that experience into either a salaried job or freelance work with more substantial publications.

5. He could explore developing a specialty in digital photography in an effort to get in on the ground floor of doing travel photos for Web magazines.

6. He could consider seeking a job as a photojournalist for a newspaper,

even if that meant starting out working in layout and working his way into travel assignments.

The more options Carlos began developing, the more creative he became in coming up with others. Before he was finished, he was generating more unconventional ideas such as:

1. Creating travel brochures and marketing materials for resorts, spas, hotels, inns, adventure tours, etc., who he could contact by networking with graphic designers and advertising agencies through professional associations he belonged to.
2. Contacting art departments of corporations in the travel industry and soliciting assignments for their marketing materials and advertising campaigns.
3. Since he was located in Burbank, California, the heart of the entertainment industry, he could explore working as an on-location photographer for movies being filmed in exotic locales.

Carlos loved the strategic options he'd generated and went to work exploring both their feasibility and their desirability.

What strategic options have you considered? What additional ones can you imagine by thinking creatively outside the norm? Who could you brainstorm strategic ideas with? What haven't you considered? The more varied options you generate to consider, the more easily you'll find the options that are best suited to your goals and your situation.

What looks like luck is often a matter of coming up with a creative strategy that suits you and your situation. Eager to free himself from a dead-end job writing computer codes, Jack happened onto a skin cream that had wonderful properties. Those who tried it saw immediate, dramatic results, so Jack decided this was his opportunity to change directions. After all, health and beauty are major trends that show no sign of abating, as baby boomers move into their 50's en masse.

The problem was, Jack had no background, contacts, or experience in the health-and-beauty industry, but he was motivated. He invested all his savings in producing and packaging his health cream and set about getting it into department stores and health food stores, but he hit one brick wall after another. Buyers were not interested. He was a tiny fish trying to get into a big pond, and he was swimming upstream. When he came to us for a strategy session, he'd been trying to peddle his cream for three years and still wasn't even near the pond.

Judy also wanted to market a health-and-beauty product. She stumbled onto it while working as a flight attendant in need of covering the dark circles under her eyes. Like Jack, she saw her product idea as an opportunity to change directions. She wanted to stop traveling and get on a more normal schedule. But she needed to support herself and daughter and didn't want to lose the freedom, flexibility, and income a flight attendant job provided. Also, like Jack, Judy had no background in the health-and-beauty field, but she took an entirely different approach.

Instead of trying to swim up the large, crowded, conventional stream into department and health food stores, Judy devised a creative strategy that capitalized on her unique situation. Using savings, she enrolled in beauty school and within six months was licensed as a facialist and started seeing clients in her home. Most of her early clients were flight attendants she'd known through her job. Of course, she applied her product under the eyes of her clients before their session ended. Soon, she had word of mouth going for her among hundreds of airline employees who started clamoring for her product. She began selling it to them through the mail. Then she created a highly personal and practical newsletter on health and beauty for her clients and anyone who expressed interest in her eye cream. She got many orders through this newsletter.

Judy also started doing skin-care seminars for airline employees and eventually wrote a book about skin care. Although Judy's cream can't be found in any store, by capitalizing upon the strengths of her situation she has created the means to a steady income based upon opportunities of the health-and-beauty field. Were she to want to expand into retail stores, the track record of success and the national following she's built over the past several years could open otherwise closed doors.

Now, getting back to Jack's situation. He wasn't any less motivated or committed than Judy. After all, he was still trying three years later, long after a less motivated person would have given up. He had also invested his savings, but he didn't have a strategy based on the strengths of his situation. In fact, in trying to sell his product to buyers, he was out of his league.

It might seem as though Judy is just better situated for success than Jack, who has no interest in becoming a facialist. Nor does he have a network of hundreds of flight attendants who need his face cream. How could he possibly be as successful as Judy? But that only appears to be the case because Judy had marshaled her existing resources and Jack had not. Once Jack created a strategy that marshaled his resources, he achieved a similar level of success that would leave a stranger thinking how ideally positioned he was to change directions.

While Jack doesn't have an interest in providing skin-care services or a built-in list of followers, the challenge of getting his product onto the market is actually why he's so motivated to do it. He loves a challenge. But to be successful, he needs a better strategy, one that draws upon his unique resources, which are:

1. Excellent computer skills
2. The ability to organize, problem-solve, and work with materials
3. Many hours spent communicating every day online
4. A wife and sister who both go to facialists

These resources position Jack nicely to sell his product on the Internet. He has the computer skills to create his own site and effectively market on the Web. He would be right at home doing a demographic analysis of those who respond in order to carve out a unique niche for himself from among an infinite range of possibilities, i.e., women over sixty-five, women who have just had cosmetic surgery, recently divorced women, professional women, men who go to manicurists, men who get facials, etc.

Finally, since his product produces dramatic results once someone uses it, he can work through what we call "gatekeepers," people who come into contact with his potential customers on a regular basis in the course of what they do. Facialists, for example, would be excellent gatekeepers for Jack, and, through his wife and sister, he already has access to at least two he can contact and offer samples of his product to. When they like the results his product provides their customers, they can become distributors. In fact, Jack could contact Judy!

Judy would be as ill-prepared to do complex demographic analysis of online sales as Jack is to giving speeches on skin care to a roomful of flight attendants. But both have existing resources that they can marshal into a creative strategy for reaching their goals.

TURBO FUEL: Strategy Sessions

To generate creative strategy options, set aside time for the kind of strategy sessions that spur you into thinking most creatively. How do you do your best thinking?

___ Talking it out with others
___ Visualizing possibilities in your mind
___ Sleeping on the issue
___ Taking a long drive or a walk
___ Writing out the issue in a free-flowing fashion
___ Other ways

Commitment: What Have You Done So Far?
What Will You Do Next?

In the process of investigating his many strategic options, Carlos had soon made progress toward his goal to do travel photography. In order to talk with people about his options, he'd created a business card and stationery that features one of his photographs as a way of introducing himself as a

135

travel photographer. He'd also pulled together a rudimentary portfolio of his best photos from personal travels. He'd developed a superb list of networking and referral contacts. But now it was time for him to narrow down his options so he could get started on a specific plan of action.

After reviewing his choices by checking in with his inner compass and carefully considering his situation, he mapped out the following strategy. He would keep his job and:

1. Specialize in scenic nature shots
2. Enroll in a photo workshop
3. Sign up for a travel tour
4. Volunteer to take publicity photos for three small nearby mountain communities
5. Talk with advertising agencies who handled resorts and travel companies to explore freelance assignments

By the time Carlos got this strategy on paper, he was committed and ready to start doing what he needed to do

Are you ready to commit to a particular strategy? To select the best one for your situation, review the strategies you're considering in detail. Imagine yourself carrying out each one. Which one feels best? Looks best? Is most comfortable? Most feasible? Most likely to succeed? Which one can you imagine yourself carrying out most willingly, reliably, and effectively? What makes you think it would work? Once you've convinced yourself, you'll be more likely to follow-through and be able to convince others to support your efforts.

Keep in mind that your strategy need not be cast in stone. Settling on a specific strategy doesn't mean you can't pursue other strategies later. You can, and should, alter your strategy as you go, based on your experiences. But you should believe in and want to pursue whatever strategy you select at a 7 or above, on a 10-point scale. If you don't, adjust it until you do.

TURBO FUEL: Answering Your Central Question

If you're not ready to commit to a specific strategy yet, ask yourself, "What is the central question I have about my situation right now? What is it I need to know?" Is there additional information you need to gather? Do you still have reservations you need to check out? How might you find the answer to this central question?

Write your central question in your journal and read over it daily. Keep it in mind. Once you recognize your central question, if you are alert to it, you will have a guiding thought or intuition about how to answer it. Coincidences will arise, or synchronistic events will occur that provide you with ideas or information. Someone you haven't seen for a long time might call or e-mail you, for example, and the conversation will provide information you can act upon to lead you toward the answer you're seeking to move on.

Do You Have a Map?

Can you complete the following statements?

"I'm ready to commit to doing _____."

"I've already done _____."

"My next step is _____."

Example:

We're ready to commit to offering Getaway for a Change workshop in Pine Mountain. We've formed the Pine Mountain Institute, gotten a DBA (Doing Business As), secured an Internet domain name, created a logo, business cards, and stationery, and developed a workshop program description. Our next step is to start marketing the seminars to begin in the spring.

Hung Up? Getting through Stage Five

"I don't know what's wrong with me," the woman said in despair, then laughed to shake off the feeling. "I know I need to make a change, but I just don't know how. I've tried. I really have. I've tried everything I can think of." Finding a workable strategy is often the point where people run headlong into a major logjam to actually being able to change directions. We can fool ourselves about whether we've faced reality, or said goodbye or found a focus, but we can't fool ourselves for long about whether we have a strategy, because if we don't have one we won't act.

It's much like the problem we face in keeping New Year's resolutions. Most people give up on their resolutions well before February 1st because they have set an intention but have no strategy for implementing it. As you'll see in the next few pages, there are at least three ways we commonly get hung up without a strategy to commit to. We get confused, we're too stubborn, or we're taking on too big a blue sky.

CONFUSION: STUCK IN A FOG

Bridgett, a single mother, just couldn't see her way to leaving her dead-end job. Although she was getting paid much less than she could command elsewhere and was unappreciated on her job, she had taken it because her employers allowed her the flexibility to take off whenever she needed to stay home to care for her handicapped son. But in working with us to develop a strategy for finding a new line of work that would free her from the financial pressures she felt, every time Bridget got a good idea, she would suddenly become quite confused. Her voice would rise and she would put her hand to her chest, as if she couldn't get enough breath and then would pretty much tune out whatever was going on, staring out in space for a minute until she relaxed.

When she had regained her composure, Bridget would point out that the ideas she'd raised just weren't something she really wanted to consider. "That just wouldn't work for me," she kept saying. "I would be too worried that . . ." At this point, she would begin talking rapidly about what she wanted, why she needed to proceed slowly, and why everything was actually fine for now.

Bridget's reaction is a common one when we feel that we're going to lose control over a situation that has happened to us again and again. We close down, focus in on what we fear could happen, overintellectualize and confuse ourselves to the point where we can't see options for doing anything differently. In Bridget's case, after her husband left her with an ill baby, she had lost several jobs because she had to take off too many days to care for her ailing child. Since she had no other means of support, each of these experiences had sent Bridget into a panic. But that had been over ten years ago.

Since her son hadn't required any emergency care in several years, Bridget didn't realize that the memory of those past traumas were preventing her from finding a workable strategy for improving her current situation. But when we saw how she kept confusing herself, we asked, "What are you afraid will happen again?" Immediately, her fears about the past came tumbling out, and we were able to begin working to develop a strategy that would provide both an income and the flexibility she needed to care for her son in the unlikely event another emergency would arise.

Is some past trauma, or traumas, preventing you from moving forward, causing you to be afraid to think clearly and decisively about new options, for fear of repeating something that has happened to you again and again? What aren't you hearing, what aren't you seeing, because you're looking at life through the lenses of past traumas?

TURBO FUEL: Find Solutions in Your Dreams

When you can't see your way out of the fog, try letting your dreams show you the way. Use this technique from Cynthia Richmond, author of *Dream Power, How to Use Your Night Dreams to Change Your Life*. Before retiring at night, ask yourself, "How could I accomplish this goal?" Write your goal out in your change journal and place it beside your bed. Then, repeat the question several times as you fall asleep: "What is the key to accomplishing my goal?" Then add, "I will remember my dreams. My dreams are important to me." When you wake up the next morning, write down anything you remember in your change journal. You may get clear, literal advice or symbolic answers to your query.

STUBBORNESS: STOP FIGHTING YOUR SITUATION

Remember, a strategy can never be any better than our understanding of the situation. If we stubbornly fight against seeing or accepting our situation, we'll never be able to come up with an effective strategy. Do you recall Jeanette, the thirty-six-year-old talk-show host who lost her job to a younger woman? Jeanette had finally been able to say goodbye to her dream role on television and move on with her life. She'd taken a job as an event coordinator to support herself while she developed a strategy for a career as either a professional speaker or a radio talk-show host. But after getting back on her feet and settling into her new job, Jeanette was stumped as to how to implement her new focus.

In serving as an emcee on her job, she had discovered that while she could pursue a career in public speak, it wasn't her passion. She wanted to focus on getting a radio talk show. After all, no one knows how old you look when you're talking on the radio. But as she began to explore possible strategies for having a radio show, she kept getting hot under the collar about the fact that she would have to court radio stations and possibly even buy the time for her own show, at first, to get established in this new medium. "I shouldn't have to approach them as if I'm just starting out," she told us. "I've had my own TV show, for Pete's sake!"

Besides, she added, she couldn't imagine herself selling commercial spots to cover the costs of having her own show. Her palms got sweaty at the very thought of it. She wanted radio stations to seek her out, but, after all her strategies to stimulate their interest came to nothing, she felt stuck.

Jeanette's reaction to her situation is a common response to fearing you don't have any options because others won't take you seriously. She didn't want to accept her situation as a newcomer in a different medium, so she wouldn't ever talk to stations about how she might meet them halfway. From her perspective, it would be better to forgo what she wanted than to risk being rejected again. It was an all-or-nothing proposition. But, actually, it was her own stubbornness that was holding her back.

Once Jeanette could accept her situation, she could see that while she might not like having to start out in a new medium, she did have assets to bring to the table that a novice didn't have. She could reach out to program managers at the stations, for example, and explore creative alternatives. This insight enabled her to kick free of her fears and approach local stations about the idea of hosting a show for thirty-something women, using her own trauma as a selling point. She found a station who agreed to give her a shot at a show, if she would help them sell commercial spots based on her reputation as a television personality, promote the show on her web site, split the ad revenue, and get paid for whatever promotional appearance fees they could arrange. Facing the best and the worst of her situation opened the door to a new beginning that she could walk through with confidence.

TURBO FUEL: Get Moving

Whenever you feel stuck, get moving. Start a running, jogging, walking, or swimming regimen for twenty to thirty minutes at least every other day. Allow your body to really get into the movement. Be sure to drink plenty of water before, during, and after your workout. One good way to assure that you're getting enough liquid is to fill a twenty-four ounce container and be sure you've emptied the bottle before you return to your normal activities after exercising.

TOO BIG A BLUE SKY: ZOOM IN

Sometimes, the change we want to make looks just too large for us to tackle. When we're looking at the whole picture of what we'd like to accomplish, it can be hard to see the details for how we could get there. But a strategy is actually a theory or an idea for how we can break down the big picture into many little, manageable pieces, like a puzzle that we can put back together as the future we intend to create. But if we've been taught that we must swallow life whole or not at all, strategizing will be a difficult process.

Take Vanessa's situation. She had always planned that someday she would own a veterinary clinic, and after graduating from college, she had been accepted to vet school, when her uncle's business ran into problems. The whole family, including Vanessa, dropped what they were doing and rallied to help save him from bankruptcy. With their efforts, the company turned around, and Vanessa stayed on to oversee the office management. After a few years, though, she became bored with her job and started to feel resentful about having given up her dream to become a vet and run an animal hospital. "This isn't me," she said of her role as an administrator for a shipping company.

Whenever she revisited the idea of pursuing her lifelong dream, however, it just seemed insurmountable. So she tried to block out her disappointment and pretend everything was fine. But her uncle could see how unhappy she was and encouraged her to explore other possibilities. What if, we proposed when she finally decided to think about it, she were to take an administrative office position in a veterinary clinic and work her way up to her dream? Or what if, now that her uncle's business was thriving, he could lend her the money to continue her education? Or, what if she could partner with several vets and together open a small clinic Valerie could promote and manage? By taking her eyes off the big picture of starting her own clinic and looking instead at smaller steps she could take toward that eventual goal, the impossible began to look like a possibility, and she could focus on finding a strategy to make it so.

Are you focusing on more than you can take on all at once and thereby feeling too overwhelmed to develop a strategy that will get you started? Is the scope of your dream preventing you from setting priorities and seeing how you could move, step-by-step, toward something more suited to who you are and what you want in life?

TURBO FUEL: Get Help

If you don't know where to begin in breaking down your goals into a manageable strategy, you need not struggle with your challenge alone. There are many experts you can turn to for help in any given field who can mentor you, including career counselors, business consultants, and personal

coaches. The best route to finding such assistance is through personal referrals from friends and colleagues, but if you can't find help that way, check
out coaching and career sites on the Web, such as www.coachfederation.org
and coachu.com.

Once you have a strategy, laid out step-by-step, that you're committed to
implementing, it's time to put your show on the road!

Breakthrough: James

James was ready for a change. He had been selling radio advertising for over
thirty years and had enjoyed this lucrative career, but he had always dreamed
of doing freelance writing. After the death of a close friend and colleague,
James realized he had better start his new career before it was too late. But
his major challenge was financial. Before quitting his job, James needed a
strategy for making the transition to freelance work. To maintain his standard of living, he needed to bring in $2,000 a month, above and beyond his
Social Security and investment income. In reviewing the options, he was
attracted to two alternatives: getting a line of credit based on the equity in
his home either (1) through a home equity loan or (2) by using a reverse
mortgage. He needed some advice on which way to go.

Since James owned his home, free and clear, either of these options
would be a workable choice. By using the reverse mortgage, he would not
need to make any payments on the money he borrowed, but the interest rate
would be higher than a home equity credit line. The longer he lived, though,
the lower the reverse mortgage interest rate would be, due to amortized up-
front loan fees. The line of credit, on the other hand, would involve making
monthly payments at least on the interest, and those payments would go up
over time, the more money he'd borrowed.

James decided that, given his age, the reverse mortgage would prove to be
the most desirable and workable strategy. Having found a way to a transition
without risking his financial security, he was excited about launching a new
career at the age of eighty-four!

CLOSING REFLECTION

What's your plan? What are you ready to commit to doing next? You don't need to push yourself to be any further along than you are. But wherever you are, you need a strategy for where to go next. It's time to act, even if it's to gather additional information or experience to help you decide on your next step. Each strategy you undertake will lead to the next one. So write out your strategy at this point and the action steps you're willing to take to implement it.

This written plan is the first physical manifestation of your future direction. It will serve as the bridge between your ideas for achieving your desires and the real world where they will come to life.

> The truth of the matter is that you always know the right
> thing to do. The hard part is doing it.
>
> —GENERAL H. NORMAN SCHWARZKOPF

6

PUTTING THE SHOW
ON THE ROAD:

EXPERIMENTING, INITIATING,
AND FOLLOWING THROUGH

We can only be what we give ourselves the power to be.
—THE CHEROKEE FEAST OF DAYS

You're tired. It's been a long day. The couch looks so inviting. The laundry is overflowing in the hamper. You haven't answered your personal e-mail in days. Dozens of demands, more or less appealing, are calling for your attention, and the couch remains the most tempting of them all. But not any of these things are part of your plan for this evening. If you're going to be changing directions, tonight is for the class you enrolled in, the résumé you're going to redo, the book you're going to finish reading, or the web search you need to do. Moments like these are the ultimate test of our commitment to change and our strategy for doing it. They are the reason we need to commit at a 7 or above on a 10-point scale. Anything short of that, and we just might not resist the couch or the laundry or the e-mail or any of the other demands life places on us.

The moment of truth comes when it's time to put our show on the road. Even if we've found a new direction we'd love to take and a strategy for getting there that suits our situation, there's still the challenge of fitting all that's involved in the making of our new life out of our old one. We have only twenty-four hours in a day and only so much energy before we have to call it a day. That's the toughest part of changing directions—you have to do it while juggling the road show you've already got up and running. Rarely do we get to just drop those balls and play with the new ones. Yet our time and our energy are the raw materials from which we will craft our new direction . . . or not.

Lydia had put her show on the road. She had it together. When she arrived at the workshop, she had her daily planner with her and referred to it often, as she described how she was implementing her plans to open a restaurant. She knew it was a long shot. She knew the 95 percent failure rate. But for her, this was not a whim, and she didn't intend to become another of those statistics. She had a strategy and had been busy implementing it for the past five years. She'd learned the ropes by managing a successful restaurant, taking courses in restaurant management and business administration, and developing a business plan. Recently, she'd obtained a loan to buy an existing well-located restaurant that was going out of business.

In addition, Lydia had interviewed the owners and carefully reviewed their books. The restaurant wasn't doing well, so she had to find out why. Over weekends and evenings, she'd called two hundred people who lived in the neighborhood at random to ask them how often they went out to eat and what types of food they liked. Based on that survey, Lydia had decided to dramatically change the name, decor, and menu of the existing establishment and offer a light cuisine instead of New York deli-style food. She was scheduled to open in two months and was getting the feedback she needed for a dynamite marketing campaign.

Earl was looking more and more dejected as he heard Lydia talking with such confidence about the steps she was taking. He could see her boundless energy building as she spoke with excitement about the results she was getting. She exuded so much enthusiasm that probably everyone in the room would have invested in the restaurant, if she'd asked them to. He, on the other hand, felt like he just couldn't get it together. He, too, had a strategy for changing directions. Tired of working as the head of the parts department for a car dealership, Earl was starting a landscaping business on the side so he could have greater flexibility and spend more time outdoors doing what he loved most—gardening. His plan was to build up his business to the point that he could phase out of his job.

"I think my success is my downfall," he explained, when his turn came to talk with the group. He'd lined up a number of customers right away but didn't have the time to do the quality work he enjoyed. He'd get out in a customer's yard, and hours later he'd still be there, even though he had other customers waiting for him. They would page him impatiently and he'd rush over to his next appointment, leaving the work he'd started incomplete. Already, several customers owed him money which he couldn't collect until he finished their projects, but he couldn't arrange to get back to finish them because he was too busy trying to handle new customers.

He thought he'd solved the problem by hiring some helpers, but they only made things worse. He was never satisfied with their work and had to do it over, putting him all the further behind and taking more money out of his pocket, which he couldn't afford. "I just can't handle it all, but I love the work," he confessed, adding that his problems had been further complicated by repeated rounds of the flu that kept him both home from work and unable to respond to his customers.

Is your life running more like Lydia's or Earl's? Are you organized and busy implementing your strategy? Are you coordinating the various aspects of your existing life so as to have the time, money, and energy to put your show on the road? Or is your situation crowded and disorganized like Earl's? Or perhaps it's more like Carla's, whose grand plans were still sitting on the back shelf of her life.

If you recall, Carla had trained for many years to become a psychologist, and, after obtaining her license, she had taken several unfulfilling positions before realizing that while she loved psychology, she didn't like practicing psychotherapy. She was, she concluded, an academic at heart and wanted to teach and write about her chosen profession. So she'd worked out a strategy. She was going to seek out a position at a community college, teach basic courses there while she wrote a book, and then work her way into a tenured position at a college or university.

Well, that was the plan and that's what it remained—a plan. When she contacted us sometime later, she was still practicing psychotherapy with a partner, still not liking her work and still wanting to find a teaching position and write a book. "I haven't made any progress," she told us, shaking her head in frustration. "Between my practice, the family, and my community projects, I just can't find the time to do what I know I need to do."

The Task: Getting Organized for Action and Getting Plans Under way

Like a river, life moves along the course of least resistance, unless consciously diverted elsewhere through concerted effort. Rivers flow along a bed. They don't diverge easily from this accustomed path, which has been their course of least resistance for hundreds and thousands of years. And so it is with any change we wish to make. Changing our lives requires effort. We have to exert an effort to restructure our lives to support the changes we want to make and provide a new riverbed along which the paths of our lives can unfold. As long as our lives are structured to function as they have, they will continue on indefinitely as they have . . . until forces beyond our control sweep our structure away and take us who knows where.

How is your life structured right now? Are your days, weeks, and months structured to assist you in smoothly putting your strategy on the road, or is every day a struggle you must endure or simply give up on?

Carla couldn't find the time to get her plans started. Earl couldn't manage the time he had. His life was, on the one hand, overly structured by his job from 8:00 to 5:00, when he had no flexibility and, on the other hand, time completely unstructured on weekends and evenings. He was initiating activities but couldn't follow through on them. To put our show on the road, we need to reorganize and structure our lives to do it all—initiate, follow through, evaluate, and revise our strategies until we've redirected our lives down a new path. We have to take charge of our time, master our energy, manage ourselves, and have a winning attitude.

TAKE TIME: SCHEDULE FOR RESULTS

Time is such a wonderful resource. As long as we're alive, it never runs out and it's totally democratic. We get a fresh supply everyday, no matter who we are or how well or poorly we've used yesterday's supply. But most of us aren't taught to think of our time as a resource. We approach it more like it was a gym bag that we stuff our lives into. We see its limitations, not its limitless malleability. As children, few of us are taught about how to use our time. It's scheduled for us, and often our decisions about how we would use it are overridden by parents, teachers, and later spouses and bosses.

Earl, for example, who was trying to get his landscaping business under way, grew up in a household where what everyone in the family did with their time was under his mother's thumb. But only inside the house. Outside, there was no supervision whatsoever. "I could do whatever I wanted," he recalled. "My siblings and I ran wild all over the neighborhood until well after dark." That behavior carried over into his school experience. "I was a great student in class, but as far as studying and homework were concerned, well, that's why I never finished college."

Now, over thirty years later, he was structuring his time the same way. On the boss's time, he was on a short leash, doing what he was told, when he was told, and expecting the same of those who worked under him. After hours, though, he was doing whatever he wanted when he wanted, and it wasn't helping his business.

What did you learn about time from your family? How is your family's history with time influencing the patterns of how you use time today?

Because Carla was juggling her own time in private practice and with a family and lots of community responsibilities, she felt like "everything's up to me and everything needs to be done right now. Sometimes there's so much to be done, I just don't do anything!" Whereas Earl needed to learn when to *stop* what he was doing so he could put first things first, Carla needed to learn where to *start* so she could put first things first. Both needed to learn how to decide what should be done now, what could be done later, and what didn't need to be done at all.

Before we can change directions, we've got to make room for the things we need to do to carry out our strategies. That means clearing away ample time, space, and energy for them. Otherwise, we end up operating on the Hope System—that is, "I hope I'll get to that," or "I hope I can fit that in," and, of course, we usually don't. Actually, worrying about all the things we have to do and whether we'll get them done is one of our biggest time wasters.

But most of us have a myriad of minutiae that is taking up far too much of our time, space, and energy. This is what we call the "backlog," and it's usually what's keeping us from getting around to putting a new show on the road. In fact, research shows that one in four of us wastes twenty minutes a day just looking for misplaced items. That's fifteen eight-hour days a year— the equivalent of a three-week vacation! Professional organizers estimate that we can save an hour a day just by cleaning out our files and piles twice a year!

So, the first thing Carla needs to do to take off some of the time pressures she's feeling is to clear out the backlog and get rid of those things in her life that she doesn't need to be doing. Here are some ideas for how to do that fast.

TURBO FUEL: Clear Your Plate

You can't concentrate on implementing your strategy if you're spending your time keeping track of all kinds of other things you could, should, and ought to be doing. To clear your mind, sit down and make up a list of everything you think you need to do—everything. Include things that you keep worrying about getting around to, like sending a birthday card to Aunt Emma, sorting your tax receipts, getting a new prescription for your glasses, replacing the broken VCR, and visiting that web site everyone's been recommending. Momentarily, this list may seem overwhelming, but having it written out where you can see it will free your mind immensely and immediately pinpoint areas you can reduce or eliminate.

As Carla looked at her list, she could see that many of the things she thought she had to do weren't getting done anyway, and weren't nearly as important as taking her life in a new direction. She could also see what was a priority and what wasn't. For example, she could and should delegate many of the activities involved in her community projects to other volunteers in the organization. She was doing lots of things for her children that they that could and should be doing for themselves. And, all the time she was continuing to invest in keeping her practice going was actually an investment in a life she no longer wanted to live. If she stopped networking to get new client referrals, for example, she would have time to start looking for an academic position.

If life is a vast ocean, and time is the vessel in which you travel through life, how would you describe your journey? Are you traveling at the helm of an ocean liner in command of the seas on a clearly charted course? Or are you on a sailboat drifting about on the winds of life—as the wind blows, so your day goes? Does your life feel more like a leaky rowboat that you're pushing, pulling, and struggling to keep afloat, or have you been thrown from the boat and are just trying to hang on to the sides, as you ride out the storms of each day?

Nothing happens until we create a space for it in our day, and that's what a schedule is for. Lydia, the woman who is buying the restaurant, has taken this to heart. She has mastered the art of scheduling. She sets goals for each day based on where she is in the process of implementing her strategy. But, unlike Earl, whose goals are more general in nature, Lydia's goals are very specific. Earl's goal for the day might be to "do a good job for as many people as possible," while Lydia's goal would be to "interview ten people by 9:00 P.M., review the last six months' expenditures by 10:00, and then relax and get to bed before 11:00."

Specific goals provide a target for us to shoot at. They enable us to focus on what we want to accomplish, and they let us know what we have accomplished and what we haven't. By treating his goals in a general way, Earl doesn't have to face up to whether or not he is on target. He can pretend all is well and enjoy the freedom of doing whatever he wants, but, as a result, he's catching himself coming and going. If he were to start setting specific goals, he would know when he's getting behind on a given job and could act accordingly. If his goal is to complete three projects per week, for example, he can be more realistic in scheduling work with new clients and be sure he has income coming in each week from the projects.

Are you setting specific goals to accomplish each day? How do you know if you've accomplished them? If you're not sure, you need to set more specific goals, i.e., the number of things you will do and when you will have them done.

You may recall that Lydia carries a daily planner with her. She lists her goals at the top of the calendar for each day. The advantage of this is that her goals are always in sight, because the human mind always goes toward what's in front of it. By keeping her goals where she will see them, Lydia rarely forgets them. Carla, the aspiring academic and writer, recognizes that's what she needs to do, too. Her goals are losing out to the other events of her day, so she started listing them on the calendar page of her daily planning program:

Goals for Today:

- ✓ Create a rough draft for the table of contents of my book
- ✓ Find someone to do the flyer for my workshop
- ✓ Visit three academic job sites

Lydia is still operating with a paper-based system, but tracking goals with software like Microsoft's Outlook or Ascend 4.0 by Franklin Quest, which Carla has started to do, is even easier because the programs automatically carry incomplete goals forward day-to-day.

There's something else about Lydia's schedule that accounts for her success. If you recall, she had been working on her strategy for five years. That's because she needed that much time to fit in gaining job experience, taking coursework, and doing research into the rest of her life. She has a family. She has friends. She has a personal life. So she needs a schedule that will allow time for all of this. Earl, on the other hand, jumped into his strategy without thinking about how it would affect the rest of his life. He wanted to take the world by a storm, so his weeknight and weekend work schedule left no time for family, social activities, or personal R&R (rest and relaxation). The result was that his health suffered, and chronic illnesses were putting him even further behind.

Look at your calendar. Does it include room for personal and family activities? Or do they have to be squeezed into the "spare" time you never have?

To make sure there is room in the day for some of everything that matters most, Lydia prioritizes her "to do list" into A or B tasks. "A's are the truly important things," she explains, "and B's are everything else." Of course, tasks related to opening her restaurant are always among her "A" priorities. Carla, on the other hand, wasn't prioritizing her activities, and those that might lead to getting a teaching position kept falling to the bottom of the list.

Ask yourself throughout the day, "What is most important to me? Am I using my time for what's most important?" There will never be time for everything there is to do, but there is always time for what's most important.

Setting specific goals with target dates, identifying action steps, setting priorities, and putting what matters most onto the calendar, as Lydia does, is by far the more accepted way to get and stay on track.

But you wouldn't have to know Jeannie very long to know that she could never follow a schedule like Lydia's. Although she's begun producing music festivals, which require a lot of detailed organization, Jeannie takes quite a different approach. While Lydia is highly linear and logical in scheduling her goals, Jeannie prefers a more intuitive, holistic approach.

Jeannie is an early bird. She arises around 5:00 A.M., gets a cup of coffee, and heads for her deck, which looks onto a forest with a briskly bubbling stream running through it. Bird feeders hang from the surrounding trees, so each morning Jeannie is greeted by a sunrise serenade of songbirds. Regardless of the temperature or time of year, Jeannie sits quietly on her deck for an hour or more and allows her day to take shape in her mind. She focuses on her intention, reviews her situation, and lets her inner compass be her guide. At the close of this meditative time, she usually joins her husband for an early morning dip in the hot tub, and then she's off for the day.

Her approach to time remains the same as the day unfolds. With her intention always in mind, she lets her inner compass guide the activities she initiates and follows through on. Although some would say her approach is far too unstructured, it works for her, and it has several key things in common with Lydia's more conventional one: They both keep their intentions clear throughout the day; they both spend their day initiating specific activities that further their goals; they both follow through on what they most importantly initiate; they both evaluate the results and learn from their experiences; and finally, they both accomplish what they set out to do.

How about you? Do you work most effectively taking a more logical, linear approach to scheduling your day? Or is a more intuitive, holistic approach most effective for you? The right schedule never feels restrictive. It frees you to put your energy into the direction you want to go with less effort. If you're always complaining about, fighting against, or ignoring your schedule, you need to develop a new one.

MASTER YOUR ENERGY: LISTEN CAREFULLY

In his excitement to get out of his job and into his landscaping business, Earl had taken on too many clients too fast. As a result, he couldn't keep up with himself. He was out of energy. Tired, exhausted, ill with reoccurring bouts of flu, he continued to drive on until his immune system broke down. He developed bronchial pneumonia and ended up in the hospital.

Earl was just beginning to recover his health when we spoke with him.

He was back at work, but his landscaping business had been on hold for two months. He looked broken and wounded, but not defeated. It was as if he were a magnificent racehorse whose jockey had ridden him too hard too often. Much like Rita. Rita was a MBA graduate intent upon climbing to the top—fast! President of her own firm by thirty was her goal, and she had a very specific strategy for getting there. She had observed others use it effectively and intended to follow in their footsteps.

Rita's plan was to assume a leadership role in her professional association, thereby garnering lots of visibility, many invaluable contacts, and a reputation as a leader in her field. The strategy was working. She had served as the local chapter president and gone on to a leadership position at the national level. Through the contacts she was making in the organization, she had been able to obtain several key clients of her own while still holding down her corporate job as a trainer.

When she was offered the chance to head up the association's annual national conference, she jumped at the opportunity. Even though she had a major contract under way with a new client and pressing deadlines on her job, Rita couldn't pass up such a great opportunity to showcase her talents to the very people she needed to take her company, full-time. But to meet the demands of her complete job, deadlines for her new client, and production of the conference, she had to burn the midnight oil for months.

On the day of the conference, she'd done it all. She'd completed the project for her client, kept up her work on the job, and the conference was clearly going to be a success. The speakers were excellent. The registration was strong. Now was her time to shine. And, of course, she would be introducing the keynote speaker and giving a speech herself on the future of the field. But when she took the podium that morning, she hadn't slept for three days straight, hadn't had a day off in three months, and had slept only four to five hours a night for the past week.

At that moment, the worst possible moment, the strain of the pace Rita had been keeping came crashing down on her. She stumbled through her introduction of the keynoter. She lost her place repeatedly during her own presentation, and, under the pressure of it all, her voice cracked nervously throughout. Fortunately, she was able to save face because people respected the fine job she had done. But what should have been a glorious victory for her was instead tinged with embarrassment.

And that wasn't the end of it. Like Earl, she became ill immediately after the conference and lost two months of work due to a kidney infection. Meanwhile, she was tying up loose ends from her hospital bed with a client she hadn't given sufficient attention to. By the end of the year, Rita was burned out on her business and was wondering if she'd crashed into her own glass ceiling.

Too much, too soon. Both Earl and Rita had ignored the signals that their exhausted bodies had been sending them for months. Granted, these are extreme examples, but not uncommon. For most of us, the toll of not managing our energy effectively and respectfully is more subtle but nonetheless important. Fatigue is the number-one symptom people complain about to their doctors. We might try to write our exhaustion off to getting older or just the normal stresses of life, but it's hard to overlook the fact that most successful people have boundless energy. That was the first thing Earl noticed about Lydia when she spoke about her goals for the restaurant. She was radiant with enthusiasm, alive with energy.

There's no way around it, fatigue is a signal that we're not managing our energy well enough, and without energy we can't get much done. Yet, changing directions does place added demands on our energy. Because life wants to move along the course of the least resistance, changing the course of our lives means overcoming that resistance and charting new territory. Doing that requires us to find a delicate balance between the energy we have available and the demands we place on ourselves.

We must become like world-class jockeys who can sense the needs of their championship racehorses, knowing when to push and when to let up, when to train and when to take a day off, when to drive ruthlessly ahead and when to rein ourselves in. Actually, slowing down to the pace our bodies can handle optimally doesn't slow down our success. One year later, for example, if Earl had taken on fewer customers and if Rita had held off a year to produce a national conference, they both would have been closer to their goals.

. . .

How's your energy level? Do you get out of bed each morning feeling relaxed, refreshed, and raring to go? Do you pace yourself throughout the day so that by the time you take off, you may want to relax, but you still have ample reserves to enjoy the evening? What's your body telling you? Are you getting enough sleep? How do you know when you're tired? What can you do to refresh and energize your mind, body, and spirit?

Research at Loyal College in Baltimore suggests that the leading cause of burnout is unrealistic expectations. Burnout occurs when the demands we put on ourselves outweigh our energy supply. Of course, it's not only taking on too much too soon that drains our energy. There can be millions of reasons we become depleted—from eating the wrong foods, to staying up too late, handling family conflicts, dealing with financial pressures, fighting traffic, having constant interruptions, or working with highly agitated and irritating people.

Carla found one thing that made a big difference in her energy level. When she started assessing why she never had the energy to start her academic job search, she realized that about 20 percent of her clients took 80 percent of her energy. So, Carla decided to refer these clients to other therapists who were better suited to meet their needs. "It felt like a weight had been lifted from me," she remembers. "When I had placed the last one of these clients elsewhere, I suddenly had more energy than I'd had in years!"

What's draining your energy? How can you restructure your life to stop this energy drain?

TURBO FUEL: For a Quick Energy Boost

When you need a lift, stop whatever you're doing, get a drink of water, sit back or lie down, and take a mininap. Or have an high-energy snack like this one:

Roasted Pears with Cheese

Peel and core four pears and cut them in halves or quarters. Place pears in a baking dish and baste with a paste of:

¼ cup apple juice
1 teaspoon Riesling vinegar
1 tablespoon maple syrup
¼ teaspoon ground allspice
¼ teaspoon apple pie spice
¼ teaspoon almond or walnut oil
Dash of sea salt

Place in the oven in an uncovered baking dish and roast at 400° for 15 minutes. Then sprinkle ¼ cup of dried cherries that have been soaked in white wine or apple juice on top of pears. Baste the pears with the juice in the baking dish and bake until tender (5 to 10 minutes, depending on the ripeness of the pears).

Serve with small slices of your favorite nonfat or low-fat cheese.

Our work and living environments can make a big difference in our energy level. Environmental psychologist Roger Barker's groundbreaking research has shown that everything—from the lighting and temperature of a room to the colors of the decor and the amount of space we have, the number of people we share it with, and the furniture we sit on—can affect our energy level. The effects of the environment throughout the day often go unnoticed, but if we want to work at our peak, we should pay more attention to how our environment is affecting us. A supportive work environment can boost our energy, help us concentrate, reduce fatigue and distractions, and increase productivity.

Creating a Supportive Work Environment

To design and furnish your work space so that it nourishes rather than fatigues or distracts you, include such things as windows, plants, artwork, music, and a selection of your favorite things. Also consider the following:

- **Lighting.** According to a Harris Poll, lighting is the number-one contributor to productivity. For best results, use natural light when possible or full-spectrum bulbs. Avoid glare, and light various work tasks appropriately.

- **Soundproofing.** Columbia University found that of all environmental factors, unwanted noise has the strongest correlation to job stress. Other studies suggest that people who work in noisy settings are more likely to become discouraged than those working in quieter environments. So find a sound level at which you can remain alert but are still able to concentrate. Mask street and other unpleasant noise with background music or a white-noise generator. Soundproof windows, doors, and noisy equipment.

- **Office furniture.** Poorly designed furniture can cause irritating aches and pains and can subtly eat away at your concentration. Furniture should be comfortable and ergonomically designed to avoid muscle strain and fatigue.

- **Aromatherapy.** Psychologists at the City University of New York have found that fragrances affect how we feel and how well we think. Peppermint, for example, stimulates productivity. Lavender and apple spice are relaxing; lemon, pine, and rosemary are energizing; rose and tangerine help reduce stress; lemon has been shown to reduce work errors by more than 50 percent. So treat your office to your favorite fresh flowers, potpourris, incense, and essential oils so you can work more productively. To find out more about how pleasant aromas can improve performance, check out www. officescents.com.

- **Color.** Dr. Alexander G. Schauss, a clinical psychologist and the director of the American Institute for Biosocial Research, has found that the colors in our environment produce strong psychological and physiological effects. For example, red is energizing; blue is relaxing; yellow stimulates thinking and creativity. When researchers painted classroom walls yellow on three sides and blue in the back, student IQ scores rose an average of 12 points, and teachers felt more relaxed.

- **Fresh air.** Plants most certainly make excellent decorative items, but NASA research has shown that the right plants can also serve as air purifiers. Placing a spider plant, a peace lily, or golden pothos in your office can literally clear the air by absorbing chemical pollutants such as ozone, formaldehyde, and trichloroethylene generated by your computer, carpet, copier, and fax machine.

MANAGE YOURSELF: TRAIN LIKE A PRO

There's probably no greater power than the power to follow through on what you say you want to do. Whether it's being able to hit a tennis ball just where you want it to go, deliver a project on time within budget, or get yourself to stop smoking, being able to count on yourself to deliver what you want to accomplish is truly a gift. But when you want to take your life in a new direction, it's also an essential skill.

Yet, how often do we make promises to ourselves, set goals, make New Year's resolutions, or swear we'll do something—or never do something again—only to let ourselves down? According to a *USA Today* report, for example, nine out of ten Americans make New Year's resolutions, but, according to studies by G. Alan Marlatt from the University of Washington in Seattle, almost four out of five people fail to follow through on them.

Of course, if you like what you're doing and you're committed to a new direction, following through on what you set out to do is less of a problem. Or is it? Aren't we usually quite sincere when we make New Year's resolutions? Don't you really want to change? So, how do you know you'll do any better with your intentions to change directions? What about the days when you don't want to do what you know you need to do? What about the things you don't like to do . . . the things you want to put off . . . the things you will get to later? The best strategy, goal setting, and scheduling in the world are useless unless you can get yourself to put them into action.

Every professional athlete or performer must face this same issue. In every game, in every match, in every contest, in every act, they must ask, "Will I be able to perform at my best upon demand?" To make sure they can, they practice, rehearse, and train every day. They go through endless repetitions of their moves or their lines until they can count on themselves to do what it takes under the pressure of a competition or a production. And that's essentially what we have to do to change directions.

But, of course, athletes and performers have coaches, directors, and managers to help them. These assistants are paid to understand their clients so well that they can inspire, motivate, energize, catalyze, outfox, outmaneuver, outwait, outpsych, or, one way or another, get their charges to do their best, precisely when they need to.

While athletes and performers have their coaches and trainers to manage them, we only have ourselves. To put a new show on the road, we have to step into the role of the trainer and serve as our own coach, mentor, and manager. In other words, you have to get to know yourself very well. You have to learn exactly what will get you going, what will calm you down, and what will help you focus. You have to know how to make sure you follow through on what needs to be done when you'd rather call it a day. You have to keep yourself going when things take longer than you expected or when you get impatient and feel like quitting.

You have to start thinking of yourself as your own protégé and notice what you respond to well and what you don't. You must learn to respect your preferences and needs and appreciate your natural abilities and limitations so you can take them into account, instead of fighting with yourself or using your energy to hide the aspects you don't like about yourself.

How well do you know yourself? Are you someone you admire and respect? Do you get along well with yourself? Or do you fight with yourself about what you will and won't do? Can you motivate yourself to do what you say you want to do?

There are actually a wide variety of ways to motivate ourselves. Marsha, for example, was intent upon becoming an event planner. She learned quickly that the best way to motivate herself was to set up incentives or prizes. "If I have something special I can work toward, I get a lot more done," she says. She entices herself with promises of rewards for reaching her goals. For instance, she once told herself that if she had a particular exhibit filled by a certain date, she would send herself to an upcoming national conference. She hit the goal and took the trip!

Diane, who has a thriving private counseling practice, is motivated by the satisfaction she gets from the work she does. All she needs to do is think about how much joy her work brings, and she finds it easy to do whatever is required to make sure she succeeds. Jeffrey, a sales trainer, knows money is what motivates him. "The more money I can make, the better I produce," he told us. Ron, a professional photographer, finds that showing everyone what he can do is what keeps him going: "So many people told me that I couldn't do this and that I'd never make it. Now, all I have to do is think about how much I want to prove them wrong, and I'll do whatever it takes."

How do you motivate yourself? Do any of these varied approaches sound familiar?

- "When things look bad, I get discouraged and don't want to do anything much. So I've learned to tell myself the positive side of whatever's happening. I point out why it's not as bad as it looks, and how it could be even better than I thought. Then I feel like working all the harder."
- "When I'm under the pressure of a deadline, I get a lot done; but without a deadline, I don't get much done at all. It's got to be a real deadline, though. I can't just make something up. So, what I do is get myself into situations that involve firm deadlines."
- "I ask myself what will happen if I don't do this, and if it doesn't look good, then I want to do it."

- "I think about the kind of person I want to be, and if I'm not living up to who I aspire to be, that's a real motivator to change. When I am living up to my image of myself, I feel good and I do what it takes to do even better."
- "Facts and figures are what motivate me. I track my progress like I'm keeping a scorecard. And I watch what my competition is doing. I like to make sure I stay out in front."

Spend some time reflecting on how you motivate yourself, and explain to yourself in a few simple sentences, like those above, what works best for you.

Knowing what de-motivates you can be as important as what does. Gil, a software engineer, discovered, for example, "If I tell myself I have to do something, it's like the kiss of death. I'll do just about anything else. And, boy, has that gotten me in trouble. Now, if I don't want to do something, I just tell myself I don't have to do it. And, usually, once I know I have the choice, I go ahead and do it, if it really does need to be done."

When Kim started her publicity business, she found she disliked doing the billing. "It's so time-consuming," she moaned. "But I think of it as dumping the money out of my pockets and counting what will be coming back to me. That gets me through it."

To discover your motivators and de-motivators, pay attention to what you complain about versus what you get excited about. What gets you down? What picks you up? Start catering to yourself as if you were a prized athlete. Don't sell yourself short or let yourself get away with less than you know you can do, but make it as easy as possible for yourself to excel.

What Motivates You?

To discover what will get you going, ask yourself the following questions. There are no wrong answers. The idea is to learn what you respond to. Listen to your responses and observe your behavior to see if it confirms your answers.

1. What makes what you're doing worthwhile? What makes it a drag?

2. What makes doing something worth the effort? What makes you eager to get it done?

3. Which spurs you to do better: compliments and positive feedback about what you've done well or criticism of your performance and feedback on what you need to improve?

4. Are you more likely to strive to prevent negative things you fear might happen? Or to work toward attaining a positive outcome?

5. Do you thrive on competition? Does the opportunity to do better than someone else spur you on or intimidate you?

6. Are you more interested in improving your own performance or achieving more than someone else?

7. Do you work better with the pressure of a deadline, or do deadlines make you clutch?

8. Do you work more efficiently when you wait until the last minute to meet your deadlines, or do you like to start early and finish ahead of time?

9. Do you like to begin with the most pleasant tasks, or do you prefer to get the worst over with first and save the best for last?

One of the important ways we motivate, or de-motivate, ourselves, is by what we say to and about ourselves. We all have a constant stream of conversation running through in our minds. At any given moment, this internal chatter, "inner dialogue," or "self-talk" is either helping us carry out our intentions or working against them. If you begin to listen to your inner conversation and observe its effects, it's amazing what you'll learn. We can change our lives by changing what we say to ourselves.

Inner dialogue, or self-talk, is one of the primary ways we coach ourselves to do what needs to be done and to do it well. Just think, for example, of the effects these two different inner dialogues might have on the entire day if you awoke to discover that you'd overslept.

Scenario 1: "Boy, are you a sleaze. You'll never get anywhere in life. Didn't I tell you you're just a goof-off? How could you have overslept again? You'll never get what you want this way. If people knew how lazy you are, no one would want to work with you. You might as well forget getting anything done today. You've already blown it again."

Scenario 2: "Oh, it's late. Did I have anything I had to do this morning? Let's look at the calendar. Oh great! I'm free. Well, I guess I can oversleep once in a while. But if I need to, I can work some this evening. At least I'm feeling more rested. I'll probably get a lot more done now. Let's see, what did I want to get done today? I think I'll get up and . . ."

Which one do you think would lead to the best results for your day?

Listening to our inner chatter will tell us what kind of coach we are for ourselves. Would a good coach be saying the things you're saying? How do you respond to your inner dialogue? Does it make you feel more confident, more effective, and more eager to do what needs to be done? Or is your self-talk working against you?

Do you actually perform better based on what you say to yourself? Or does it erode your performance?

It's especially useful to notice what you say to yourself in response to problems or difficulties you encounter. If, for example, achieving a particular goal is harder to achieve than you thought, or some part of your strategy isn't working out, what do you say to yourself about that? If you don't want to do what needs doing, what do you tell yourself? If you make a mistake, what kind of comment do you make to yourself about that?

The conversations we have with ourselves at times like these are like the pep talks a coach gives his or her team at halftime. It's important to notice if our pep talks are working. Do they send us back in the game more committed and determined to succeed? Or do they send us into an emotional sinkhole? Do we go back in with an angry attitude and a chip on our shoulder? Or do we have a greater desire to excel? Do we hit the court running or do we drop out?

Being able to be give a great pep talk to yourself is a valuable skill when you're changing directions. Think of what you need to hear and tell that to yourself. Find stories that will inspire and encourage you. Look for incidents, quotes, lyrics, or ideas that will help you proceed with confidence and resolve. Write or clip them in your Change Journal.

What Do You Do When You Don't Feel Like Doing What You Need to Do?

What do you do with yourself when you know what you need to do but you don't want to do it? Here are several avenues to consider. Ask yourself:

1. What do you want to do now? Sometimes, you're perfectly willing to do a particular task at a later time; you just don't want to do it now.
2. When would you be willing to do it?
3. Do you still want it to be done? If not, why not? Does it really need to be done?
4. Are you willing to live with the consequences of not doing it?
5. What would you be willing to do? Sometimes, there is part of what needs doing that you are willing to do, and once you get started, you may find that's all it takes to get you going.
6. How else could it get done? You may find yourself having plenty of energy and interest, for example, in arranging for someone else to do it.
7. How will you feel once you've done it? Sometimes, the prospect of having it done will activate you.
8. Why don't you want to do it? Sometimes, you can alter aspects of what needs to be done to make it more appealing.
9. What would make you want to do it?
10. How long would you be willing to do it? Sometimes, you may be willing to do just a little bit at a time. If all else fails, just get up and do it!

ADOPT THE RIGHT ATTITUDE:
CHECK YOUR PREMISE

Obviously, we need more than a positive attitude to succeed. We need the skills, abilities, and strategies to do what needs to be done to get the results we're seeking. But just as we have to restructure our time, our energy, and how we manage and relate to ourselves, we may also need to restructure our attitudes about what we expect to get, as Terry's and Carolyn's experiences illustrate. They are both accountants who were working for large firms before deciding to set up their own independence practices. Although they hadn't met each other, they belonged to the same professional organization, which is how we happened to meet them at one of the annual meetings.

Earlier in the week, Terry had met with the chief financial officer of a medium-sized company. She was excited, because if she could get their business it would be her largest account and would cover her basic operating expenses for the first year. In relaying the experience to us, she revealed the thoughts that must have been racing through her mind as she drove to that meeting:

"You know, these big companies are a man's world," Terry pointed out to us nervously, her chest rigid from holding her breath. "It's so hard for a woman to be taken seriously in this field. They always treat me like I'm a little crumb on their table. They're probably already locked into using some large accounting firm. I sure hope I was able to crack their armor, but I doubt it." We could still hear the anxiety in her voice and the underlying hostility she had undoubtedly been feeling during the meeting.

Carolyn, also, had an important meeting earlier that week with a prestigious potential client. But as we listened to her story, we were struck by how different her attitude toward the meeting was from Terry's. "This was the chance I'd been waiting for!" she exclaimed, her exuberance spilling over into her words. "Everything I've done in the past five years has prepared me for that meeting. I know the industry figures. I know their position in the marketplace. There is so much I can do for them! They know they'll be working with me personally, not some junior partner or intern. I think I'll get their business."

The contrast between these two professionals' attitudes was especially dramatic because we heard these disparate views within a period of only a few minutes. Do these two women live on the same planet? How could a nearly identical situation be such a struggle for one person and such an opportunity for another? Their attitudes were showing, and most likely had influenced the outcomes of their meetings.

All our attitudes, assumptions, and expectations affect the way we experience everything we encounter. In fact, the *premise* from which we start any given action will not only color our feelings about it but also contribute significantly to its outcome. If we've perceived a situation inaccurately, we'll be prepared and ready to respond to something quite different from the situation at hand. But because our perceptions are colored by the premise from which we approach it, it's easy to misperceive a situation. Terry, for example, perceived companies as having a bias against both women and small practices like hers, so she went into the meeting at a disadvantage. Carolyn perceived herself as having something special to offer because she was a small company and therefore expected a positive response.

By paying attention to and even presetting your premise at any given moment, you can totally alter your emotional reality, your behavior, and your results.

In other words, our attitudes can go a long way in determining both our experience and our results. This doesn't have anything to do with being dishonest or denying your real feelings; it has to do with focusing on the best aspects of a given situation.

If Terry had been listening to her negative, self-defeating premise, for example, she could have looked for evidence that would support her starting from a new more positive, self-affirming position. Hearing her view—"This is a man's world"—she might ask herself, "Are there any successful women in this field?" And, of course, she could have found out that there are, by talking to Carolyn and other successful women accountants. She could then have adjusted her premise to include the thought, "Well, if they're doing well, perhaps I can, too." Even if she didn't know any successful women accountants, she could have adjusted her premise to achieve a better result by asking herself if she knew of others who had successfully done something against the odds and concluded that "If they could do what they did, I can do this."

So, as you go about carrying out any part of your strategy, check your premise first. What are your expectations? Your assumptions? Do they fit the actual situation? Will they assist you in accomplishing what you're seeking? If you're not getting the results you want, how could your premise be interfering with your success?

Are You on Track?

If you're following your plan, observing the results, measuring your progress, and adjusting your strategy accordingly, you should be on track. Check your progress here:

- Are you taking specific steps each day or each week to implement your strategy? They don't need to be major steps to count, just relevant ones, i.e., making a phone call, searching a web site, sending a letter, ordering a book, signing up for or going to a class. The goal is to initiate purposeful action of some kind to implement your strategy.
- Are you following through on the activities you initiate? Often, we get stuck after initiating a good idea by dropping the ball. We don't call back. We don't send out requested materials. We don't finish what we started.
- Are you seeing measurable progress? Have you completed a course and thereby gained skills you didn't have before? Have you read a book that has given you access to resources you need to take the next step? Have you made a contact that has produced leads or other key information you need?
- Are you any closer to changing directions? How do you know whether you are closer? How much closer are you? Can you feel a forward momentum developing? Or are you going nowhere or running into too many closed doors?

- Does your strategy need revising? If you're initiating ample activities toward your goals but have yet to make any measurable progress, you may need to revise your strategy. What is your experience telling you?
  - ✓ Have you been operating on some misperceptions or false assumptions?
  - ✓ Are there other steps you need to take that you haven't considered?
  - ✓ Is your strategy taking more time and energy than you anticipated?

TURBO FUEL: Your Results/Intention Ratio

Chart your progress using this results/intention ratio. How close do your results come to your intentions?

Intention—Results Ratio

List your intended outcomes below	No Progress: Score 0	Some Progress: Score 25	More Progress: Score 50	Accomplished: Score 100	Better than Expected: Score 110
1.					
2.					
3.					
4.					
5.					
6.					
7.					
8.					
9.					
10.					

Total your scores; then divide by the number of outcomes you have chosen. How are you doing?

Hung Up? Strategy on Hold?

More people get hung up on implementing their strategy than at any other stage in changing directions. As we said, it's the moment of truth, the point at which we move past talking and planning and wishing and hoping into actually doing. Some people, like Lydia, are born doers. They may have difficulty planning and strategizing, but when it comes to doing, they're ready to plunge in with gusto. But others of us aren't so lucky. We like planning and wishing and daydreaming, but we're too weary, scared, busy, or overwhelmed to actually do anything to manifest our dreams, especially if complications and logjams develop . . . which they inevitably do.

How about you? Are you a doer or a dreamer? Or maybe a little of both? Are you moving ahead with your strategy or are you blocked?

When we're motivated, clear on a strategy that fits our situation, and organized for action, we should be able to move ahead. But sometimes our progress gets blocked, and we must take a look at why and what we need to do to free ourselves. There are many reasons we give ourselves for why we can't proceed. The most common we hear in order of frequency are listed in the box below.

Common Blocks to Change

Where do you get blocked or bogged down in making the changes you want in your life and your work? Do you still have a clear vision of where you want to go? Can you hold on to it, through thick and thin? Do you get down to work on what needs to be done? Can you organize and coordinate all the elements of moving from where you are to where you're headed? Do you stick to business and persevere? How does life intervene to slow down, delay, or block your efforts?

Review the following common blocks to change and check any you're experiencing, or might expect to experience, based on your efforts to make changes in the past. Add other blocks that come to mind and select what you consider to be the top three blocks that might impede your progress.

THE TOP TEN MOST FREQUENT BLOCKS

____ **Fear.** Can you commit with confidence to making the changes you want and consistently and persistently focus your energy on your desires?

____ **Money.** Do you have the financial resources to support yourself while you make needed and desired changes? Are you able to finance those changes?

____ **Being overwhelmed.** Can you organize, coordinate, and manage the many elements of your daily life to support the changes you're wanting to make?

____ **Self-Doubt.** Do you believe you can have what you want and can maintain a confident, positive attitude about your prospects of getting it, throughout whatever time it takes to make the changes you desire?

____ **Time.** Can you make the time you need for the activities you must undertake in order to get where you want to go?

____ **Energy.** Do you feel energized, motivated, refreshed, and invigorated each day, so you can carry on with your life and institute the changes you want and need to make?

____ **Confusion.** Do you have a clear vision you can hold in your mind consistently as to where you want to go next? Can you imagine clearly how you'll get there?

____ **Discounting.** Can you sense when you're on and off track and make needed corrections immediately? How consistently are you able to remove negative and harmful elements from your life?

____ **Support.** Do you have support from family, friends, and colleagues for making the changes you want to make? Is there a ready supply of people who need, see the value of, and will pay for what you have to offer in pursuing your new direction?

____ **Other:** _____

_____

_____

_____

_____

YOUR TOP THREE POTENTIAL BLOCKS

1. _____

2. _____

3. _____

While these concerns are very real, they're also very common. They plague us all, from time to time. We address them in different stages through the book and in detail in the appendix, *A Guide to Handling the Emotions of Change*. The question is, why do they become major blocks to action for some, while remaining simply irritating problems to be solved for others? Usually, one or more of three underlying causes turn common problems into future-threatening roadblocks: (1) procrastination, (2) not knowing what to do when things don't go according to plans, and (3) getting discouraged and wanting to call it quits.

PROCRASTINATION: NOT GETTING AROUND TO IT

Carla, if you recall, didn't like practicing psychotherapy, but she had a strategy to seek out a position at a community college, teach basic courses there while she wrote a book, and then work her way into a tenured position at a college or university. But that was some time ago. Now, despite the fact that she'd gotten a daily planner, referred out clients that taxed her energy, and started setting specific daily goals, most of what she set out to do to change directions, like redoing her résumé, remained unfinished, and she was still making little progress. "I just can't seem to get myself to do what I need to do! But I have to do something. I'm driving my family crazy, biting their heads off, flying off the handle, and getting upset about the pickiest of things," she confessed.

Carla was suffering from chronic procrastination—she was putting off taking action on what she said she wanted to do. Before she could get her plans off hold, she had to find the underlying cause for her continuing delay. Usually, we don't know why we keep procrastinating, so to get past our inaction we have to track down the cause, detective-style. Carla considered the following typical reasons people procrastinate and their antidote:

- **Fear.** In their book *Procrastination: Why You Don't Do It, What to Do about It*, Jane Burka and Lenora Yuen say the major cause of procrastination is fear. Whether it's fear of success, fear of failure, or fear of change, when we're afraid to act, we procrastinate. Finding out what we fear, and then deciding whether it's realistic, or how we could handle things if our worst fears came true, can free us to take action. The appendix, *A Guide to Handling the Emotions of Change,* provides the tools for doing this.
- **Perfectionism.** In the face of impossibly high standards, we're likely to put off what we doubt can be accomplished. To avoid procrastinating, we need to think "performance," not "perfection." We must set reasonable standards and accept our best efforts as good enough to proceed, knowing we will improve with the experience of our continuing efforts.
- **Overwhelming tasks.** Procrastination can be the result of having set goals that we perceive as beyond the scope of our abilities. Even with a strategy in mind, if our goals are too high for us to tackle with confidence, then we will resist pursuing them. In situations like this, we need to break down our goals into shorter milestones we know we can carry out successfully and build a track record of success from which to take on even more.

- *Unpleasant tasks.* Of course, if we dread doing something, we're likely to procrastinate about doing it. But, as we've said, change takes effort, and sometimes that effort involves doing things we don't enjoy. We may need to confront people, situations, and issues we'd rather not deal with. We will probably have to do some tasks we'd as soon not do. To change, we have to focus on the outcome and how good we're going to feel once we've made the changes we're seeking.

- *Creating pressure to perform well.* Some people are motivated by crisis and pressure, so they procrastinate until the last minute and then dramatically carry out what needs to be done at the last moment. Since this strategy actually helps them do what they need to do, such individuals are usually confirmed procrastinators. The emotional cost of this approach, however, can be great and may detract from the kind of consistent, concentrated effort that making a major change of directions requires. Motivating ourselves to meet minideadlines at a reasonable pace will be far less stressful than working oneself into a panic and doing it all in one last-ditch effort.

- *Waiting until . . .* Another way we become entrenched in procrastination is by waiting for the right moment to start. Usually, there is no "right moment." If we tell ourselves we can't get started until something else has happened, it probably won't happen. "I'll do this as soon as . . ." becomes an immobilizing trap, like saying you'll go to the gym as soon as you lose weight. The way out of this trap is to start now. Now is not only the right moment; it's the only moment. Tomorrow has a way of never coming, so we must start today.

- *A red flag.* Sometimes, procrastination is a signal that what we thought we wanted to do is not the right thing to do, after all. Joyce, for example, was trying to launch a career as a potter, but when a customer offered to buy one of the largest and most beautiful pots in her small collection, Joyce kept putting her off. After much delay, she finally realized that if she sold this pot, she wouldn't be able to duplicate its unique and unusual finish. She needed it as a model. Once she realized this, she knew why she'd been procrastinating and immediately called the customer and offered to make a new pot just for her.

How about you? Is procrastination holding you back? What's the underlying cause behind your delays?

In considering why Carla was procrastinating, she realized there were a number of factors. First, her husband didn't really want her to change what she was doing, and she hated to displease him. He hadn't finished college, so she was concerned he might feel threatened by the idea of her becoming an author and a professor. If she were to put any part of her strategy into action, she just might actually be offered a new job or book contract, and there was sure to be a conflict. Her husband was somewhat domineering, so she'd always pretty much gone along with his wishes. She'd never really stood up to him before.

As a result, Carla kept losing touch with her inner compass, until she started to feel so miserable that she'd start planning again for how to make a change. Working on her plans would make her feel better, but, fearing a confrontation when it came time to implement them, there was always something else she needed to do, and she'd settle back into life as usual until she became too miserable again. She could see that it had become a vicious cycle.

But now Carla had a choice. Once she saw the pattern, she knew she either had to face the situation or continue enduring work she disliked. She summoned the courage to discuss her plans with her husband and, sure enough, he was not happy. But by being clear about the toll her work was taking on her and by staying focused on her passion, she was able to communicate the urgency of the matter to him in such a way that he wanted to support her in doing what was best for her.

Breakthrough: Carla

Once Carla had taken this stand for her own priorities, she set about refining and following through on her strategy.

- Since competition for faculty positions is fierce, she decided to work on building her credentials in order to be better positioned for a community college appointment.

- The book she had been planning to write, which was to be addressed to the general public, would have been ideal for increasing her visibility as a therapist and attracting more private psychotherapy clients. But experts advised her that publishing a more academically oriented book would boost her chances for a tenured track position, so she decided to work instead toward getting a contract to have her dissertation published.
- Meanwhile, she also started writing articles for refereed professional journals. These articles would serve two purposes. First, they were valuable additions to her curriculum vitae, and second, she could pull them together into a syllabus for her classes.
- Since teaching skills were another important academic hiring criteria, she signed up as a part-time lecturer at several community colleges. This also positioned her to know about upcoming vacancies for full-time positions.
- Finally, she started cutting back her practice to allow more time for both writing and teaching.

Carla realized it might take a year or more to implement her strategy, but by working it a little every day, she could feel the forward momentum, and it kept her motivated and focused on her long-term goal. Also, since the strategy itself resulted in fewer client hours and more teaching and writing hours, the steps she was taking to implement it were already changing the quality of her life for the better.

How Do You Avoid Doing What You Need to Do?

If you're avoiding important tasks, identify what you're doing instead, and cut off your escape routes, so you can discover why you're stuck and get your show on the road. There is a myriad of ways we avoid moving ahead with our plans. What diversions are you most apt to use?

- *Socializing on the phone*
- *Visiting with others*
- *Watching TV*
- *Starting later, stopping earlier*

- *Daydreaming and planning a glorious future*
- *Worrying but not acting*
- *Working on other less important projects*

- *Cleaning out all the file cabinets*
- *Surfing the Net*
- *Sleeping*
- *Other_____*

IT'S NOT WORKING: BEING FLEXIBLE IN THE DARK

Darnelle wanted to work in animated computer design, but she had no background in the field. She dove madly into implementing her strategy through taking courses, reading books, talking to everyone she knew, and following every lead. But then she hit a snag. She just wasn't getting in the door. She was stumped and couldn't seem to go any further. Darnelle's situation isn't uncommon. Usually, when we begin implementing a strategy, we run into factors and situations we hadn't expected, and it may look like we've hit a dead end. Sometimes, like Darnelle, we overact, and our response isn't helpful.

Darnelle's response was to quit her job, thinking this would force her to be more creative and enable her to work all the harder toward her goal. She gave a month's notice, and as the days passed, the pressure began to build. She became more demanding and strident in her contacts with potential employers and those who might help her, calling them incessantly and pressing for decisions. By the time she called us, she was emotionally distraught, living on coffee and near the point of exhaustion.

"What would happen if you stopped trying to control this situation?" we asked her. "What if you just relaxed?" "I can't," was her rapid response. "I'll be out on the street." As we talked, however, Darnelle began to see that she was the one who had created the pressure she was under, and she'd been doing this all her life—fearing the worst, driving herself to prevent it from happening, forcing the issues, and inadvertently causing the very thing she feared most.

Of course, we all have time and money pressures to contend with, but we need to give change, and the new future we want, a chance to develop. If we try to control it, we lose it. It throws us. Instead, we must be flexible, especially when we don't see the next step yet. We may need to alter our timetable, change our strategy, or find a new one that works better.

Until we give up trying to force and control the future according to our plan and our timetable, we'll never know what it might have been. If we get too attached to our intention and the time frame we place on it, based on our assessment when we started out, we may overlook the nuances and opportunities that would show us what we need to do next. We may get ahead of ourselves, thinking the picture we had of our intention is the one and only, instead of letting our exploration of its possibilities evolve into what they can actually become.

We asked Darnelle what she could do to relieve the pressure she's putting on herself so that, instead of having to make something happen, she could let something happen from her already considerable efforts. She decided to talk with her boss about staying on for a while and he was delighted. She could stay as long as she liked.

With this pressure removed, Darnelle could move from worrying about what she couldn't make happen to wondering about what could happen. Her search became more fun and less driven. Several months later, she made contact with a programmer who was launching a new web business and needed an animator. He couldn't pay her until revenue started coming in, but since she could work with him on the side, she was able to get involved and, within a year, not only was she working as an animator but she had three new animators working under her!

Like Darnelle, do you feel like it's all up to you but that you're in the dark as to what else you need to do? Often, the answers you're seeking lie around the corner ahead. What can you do to give yourself time to turn the corner and let your future unfold?

TURBO FUEL: Coffee Substitutes

If you're feeling wired and stressed out, instead of drinking more coffee or caffeine-laced soft drinks, drink fewer or eliminate them altogether. Switch instead to herbal or green teas, grain coffees, diluted fruit juices, or noncarbonated spring water. Caffeine provides an adrenaline rush but ultimately leaves you all the more exhausted. Try some of the exotic herbal and green tea selections from the Republic of Tea at www.republicoftea.com (800) 298-4TEA or Stash Tea at www.stashtea.com (800) 547-1514.

What to Do When You Don't Know What to Do

When changing directions, even with the best of strategies there will be times when you don't know what do. But that doesn't need to stop you. Here's what to do instead:

1. *Acknowledge it's okay not to know.* The first step to discovering anything is admitting you don't know but would like to.

2. *Assume something effective can be done.* No matter what situation you're in, if you start from the premise that problems are solvable you'll get much further.

3. *Let your gut guide you.* Trust your inner sense of knowing, that inner voice you always wish you'd listened to after the fact.

4. *Focus your attention away from the problem.* Instead of focusing on the problem and all its complexities, focus on your desired outcome and work backward to figure out how to get there from where you are.

5. *Generate multiple possibilities.* Usually our second or third idea is better than the first. Don't censor silly solutions; they may lead to the most effective ones.

6. *Grapple and let go.* Put your subconscious mind to work on solutions. Often the best solutions come "from out of the blue," after we've worked on them.

7. *Get help; talk it out.* Talk through the situation with others. Sometimes the process of explaining what you're thinking leads almost magically to the solutions you're seeking. Or surf the Web for ideas or inspiration.

8. *If all else fails, act.* When it's time to do something, take your best shot, then observe and learn from the results.

GIVING UP: SHOULD YOU THROW IN THE TOWEL?

"I just can't do this anymore," Kirk explained. "I've had it!" He was trying to get out of his job in customer support and into his own web business, but he had overestimated what advertisers would pay for the information he was offering and how long it would take to attract the level of visitors that would produce better ad revenues. At first it had been fun, but working long days at the job and long nights on the business had become a dizzying pace. His head was swimming, and he was losing his ability to concentrate. "I'm just under too much pressure," he admitted. "It's like trying to run in quicksand, and I want out."

Kirk was going through what many of us experience when our strategies don't go as we expect. Instead of continuing to push ourselves all the harder, like Darnelle, to force the future into compliance with our plans, some of us start to feel like throwing in the towel. Actually, most people who set out to change directions entertain the idea of quitting or doing something else at some point. In fact, it's important to allow ourselves the option to quit. Otherwise we become enslaved to our goals.

So we encouraged Kirk to take his feelings seriously, but, before giving up on his dream we suggested that he look carefully at why he was feeling as he did. He could be experiencing any of the typical reasons people have for wanting to throw in the towel:

- *It's break time.* Often we feel like giving up when we're overly tired out, burned out, or bummed out. When this is the situation, it's time to take a break, to get some sleep, take a long weekend, or go on vacation. Once we're refreshed, we can re-evaluate whether we still feel like quitting.
- *Dislike for what's involved.* There's almost always more than one way to do something, so if we hate what's involved in the way we're pursuing our goals, we should explore other ways of approaching them before throwing in the towel completely. We need to ask: "If I could do this exactly the way I would want to, how would I do it?"
- *It's not what you thought.* Sometimes, as we get into making a change, we realize it's not at all like we thought it would be, and we need to find

another more suitable direction. We shouldn't consider this a failure any more than we would if we were trying on a new shirt and decided it didn't fit right or that we just didn't like it.

- *You feel like a failure.* If the effort involved in changing directions becomes too hard or is taking too long, it's easy to feel like we're failing. Instead, it means we need to take an objective look at what we're doing. It's time to check in with our inner compass again and ask, "How much do I want this? How long I am willing to continue? Do I still want to proceed, but not at such a breakneck pace? Do I need to be more realistic? Do I need to slow down? Or have I been slacking off and need to work harder?"

As Kirk reviewed his situation, we realized he was badly in need of a break, so he and a friend took off for a long weekend at the beach. They played golf, went snorkeling, and didn't think or talk about the Web business. He didn't even take his laptop computer or his cell phone. Once he got back, he had a much clearer perspective on his situation. He really didn't want to give up on his Web idea, but he did want it to be fun again, and that meant letting go of his one-year-to-profitability goal. Kirk decided that if he was enjoying his business, it didn't matter how large or successful it became. He could keep his job and just enjoy doing it for a couple of hours a night.

Of course, not everyone would have made the same decision Kirk chose. Someone else might have decided to pursue a different Web concept or to seek venture capital to speed up the process. But Kirk adjusted his pace to the level where he felt comfortable, which is exactly what each of us must do.

CLOSING REFLECTION: Regulating the Pace of Change—The Five/Five Plan

*A*re you still committed to putting your new show on the road? Are you proceeding at the right pace for you? What is your best pace? Be realistic. Consider your situation. Do you need to be on a Fast Track, Medium Track, or Slow Track?

Whatever your choice may be, get yourself on the following Five/Five Plan. Start now. If you want to be on a Fast Track, kick up your effort. Initiate five *things and follow-through on five things every day to get your new direction under way. If a Medium Track is more suitable for you, initiate five things and follow-through on five things every week. If you'll do better on the Slow Track, initiate five things and follow-through on five things every month.*

Once we have a new show on the road, it's only a matter of time before the last vestiges of the past fade into history. Your days take on a new shape and form, as their contents are gradually replaced with the activities of life that are your new direction. What you've known becomes your "used-to-be's," and your future becomes your "now."

> *The future is uncertain . . . but this uncertainty is at the*
> *very heart of human creativity.*
>
> —ILYA PRIGOGINE

CLOSING:

NEXT!

We are each but a million butterflies
changing colors day by day.

She was a corporate executive and a mom, living in a northern California suburb when we met her several years ago. A divorce and family tragedy had turned her life upside down, and she was forced to change directions. "I'm no longer the person you knew back then," she e-mailed us recently. "Like a caterpillar, the inner core of my being has taken me on the ride of a lifetime without asking my permission. Although I had no choice but to change, I've played a role in determining my new direction, and since we last spoke, all the colors on my wings have changed."

She had traded her life in the suburbs for a mountain cabin in the forest, her Armani suits for flannel shirts, and her high-tech office for a garage filled with antique crystal and glass. "It's hard to put a label on the person I've become," she went on to explain, "but if I had to give it a try, I'd say I'm a mountain woman and collector who sells antique craftsmen glassware."

She'd attached a photo to the message, and indeed we might not have recognized her. She was sitting on the floor, amid her cherished collections. Her short, neatly cropped hair had grown long and fell in a wild cascade of curls over her shoulders. Her smile, once a perky professional grin, had become a quiet, radiant glow.

"But now, all this is changing, too," she went on to say. "I'm packing my collections for sale or giving them away, because tomorrow, I'm moving to the tiniest of cottages by the beach to produce exhibits for a major auction company. I'm crying as I pack each box," she admitted, "but I don't know whether it's from the excitement of all I have to look forward to or the pain of all I'm letting go of.

"I love the person I've become and the mountain lifestyle I've created. I'm stronger and more content," she added. "I would never have chosen the events that forced me to change from the person I was, but I appreciate their gifts. And now, my wings are about to change colors again. I'm moving on to a life that will be as different from how I live now as it has been from how I was living when you met me. But this time, I'm not afraid because I've done this before. Although it will be totally different, as you say, the steps are at heart the same, and I've made friends with them."

While we are always more than where we've been, where we are, and where we're going, each major change in directions that we make does change us. Whether we're a:

- Forest ranger turned poet
- Politician returning to the practice of law
- Talk-show host moving from television to radio
- Ex-doctor's wife resuming her medical practice
- Youth counselor becoming a flying instructor
- Mortgage broker opening a yoga studio
- Journalist turned business consultant
- Textbook editor taking writers on retreats to Italy
- Aerospace engineer turned professional photographer
- Graphic designer illustrating children's books

- Podiatrist opening a medical transcriptionist service
- Psychologist becoming a college professor

Or a million other possibilities. When we change directions, we become at least a little more of who and where are. We change, and our lives change. Then, before we know it, we change again . . . and again . . . and again. Perhaps it hasn't always been so, but it is now. When we lived a lifetime of but a few decades, we might have but a few transformations, but now that we can expect to live for many decades, we can expect to transform ourselves many times in a lifetime.

Understanding change, welcoming its intrusion—for it is always intrusive—and guiding our lives through its stages has become a survival skill as important to master as any other life skills. As this new millennium unfolds, how we greet the changes foisted upon us, as well as those that grow from within us, will have more influence over the nature and quality of our lives than virtually any other force. Yet, we'll always feel somewhat ambivalent toward change, because it means we must face things about ourselves and our lives that we'd rather not see. It means we must say goodbye to things we've valued. It means we must exert effort we might prefer not to expend. It means we must invest time we might choose to spend elsewhere. And, most of all, it means we can influence, but never totally control, the nature of our future.

But change also means discovering new possibilities we couldn't have imagined. It means the melting of confusion into the mystery of surprise and delight. It means labor expended emerging into the satisfaction of creation. It means decay and decline reversed by rebirth and renewal. It means that life, our life, is not at an end, but continues on. And so it is that we ride willingly, or are dragged reluctantly, along by the river of change. We close this book with one wish—that we each might embrace the journey of change, rise to its challenges, and participate fully in directing the unfolding of the shared future we will all call tomorrow.

APPENDIX

A GUIDE TO HANDLING
THE EMOTIONS OF CHANGE

Most people don't know it's possible to enjoy . . . all their
emotions. The key lies . . . in the emotions themselves.
Each emotion is a slightly different riddle that has embedded
within it the clues you need to benefit from it.
—LESLIE CAMERON-BANDLER

Changing directions is an emotional experience. There are invariably moments of soaring exhilaration, intense apprehension, overwhelming opportunities, paralyzing fear and doubt, gut-wrenching disappointments, and unbelievable elation—all punctuated with periodic moments of deep satisfaction, unbearable impatience, temporary rejection, alternately devastating and delightful surprises, fleeting frustrations, intriguing curiosity, and a growing sense of anticipation, confidence, and self-assurance.

In the midst of change, we may be living every day on the edge of our greatest fears and our grandest hopes. So much is at stake: our ego, our self-confidence, even our very survival may seem to hang in the balance from day to day. Any day can bring a big break. One phone call can make our week, our month, or even our year. Or the same call can be a cancellation, a rejection, or a bad turn of luck that crushes our budding hopes. And there's so much to prove. There are all the people who believe in us, the people we don't want to let down, the people who've said we can't do it, and the people who have discouraged us from trying. We're determined to show them all that we can do it. And then, of course, there's ourselves—the part of each of us who believes we can do great things and the part of us who doubts our abilities; the part that's confident and the part that's concerned.

The bigger and more dramatic the change, the more of an emotional workout it puts us through. But that's good, because if we pay attention to our emotions instead of trying to avoid them, they can be our best possible guides for navigating the tides of change. Studies in a wide range of fields, from psychoneuroimmunology to management theory, are now demonstrating that our emotions, even those we think of as negative, are designed to serve as physiological road signs pointing us toward the most appropriate action and supplying us with precisely the quality and quantity of energy we need to take, whatever action is called for.

In other words, even our "negative" emotions can be tools for positive change, instead of roadblocks to what we want to accomplish. With this in mind, the following guide identifies the useful messages and the valuable energy to be garnered from the top fifteen so-called negative emotions most people experience while trying to change directions. It's meant to serve as a roadmap for times when you don't like the way you feel and yet you're stuck with a particular emotion, going nowhere or using its energy in a self-defeating way. This guide is designed to be used at any stage in the process of changing directions. It describes the positive role each of these emotions plays in our ability to change successfully and provides specific steps for how to use the energy of each emotion to move ahead in a positive direction.*
Emotions appear in alphabetical order for easy reference.

---

*The concepts in this guide are based upon the work of many people, some of whose books or programs are listed at the end of this appendix. They include Leslie Cameron-Bandler, Michael Lebeau, Richard

Anger

Anger is a sign that you perceive some harm or threat to your well-being. It signals that you need to take action to protect yourself by stopping or preventing something dangerous from happening. If you have already suffered in some way, your anger is telling you to take action to correct an injustice or damage that's been done to you, or to take action to prevent it from occurring again. Anger can also be a sign that you believe some important standard or value of yours has been violated or that some wrong has been done.

It is an intense, fast-paced emotion. It brings on a rush of energy, enough to make sure you can safeguard yourself from any further insult or attack. The value of all this energy is lost, however, if you repress it or just flail around in it, yelling and carrying on ineffectively. We've all seen people sit on or stew in their anger or yell pointlessly at an offending situation. You've probably done it yourself at some point. Most of us have. Whether you feel like yelling at yourself or someone else, anger is meant to be put to productive use. It's not meant to be buried or endlessly flailed around in. It's meant to produce positive results. Anger sends a message "Back off! Shape up! See to it this doesn't happen (again)!"

Denying anger doesn't neutralize it. Research shows that chronic unresolved anger, whether turned inward or expressed ineffectively, has many negative health consequences, from high cholesterol levels to addictive behavior, heart attacks, and other diseases. The key is to learn how to use the potent energy that anger brings to resolve transgressions and prevent them from happening again.

Anger is never a comfortable energy to experience. It's not supposed to be. Making someone else feel sorry or feel miserable is rarely a sufficient result, however, especially in a career situation where your ability to achieve your goals depends on having a positive reputation and getting others to support and assist you. To be effective, anger must be used in a way that

---

Bandler, and John Grinder, all pioneers in the field of neurolinguistic programming; Gene Bua, director of Acting for Life; endrocrinologist Deepak Chopra; psychologist and neuroscientist Daniel Goleman; psychologist and brain researcher Robert Ornstein; and psychologist Dean Allen, creator of the BodyTalker™ system.

makes things better, not worse. It should enable people to know what you expect of them and that they can't cross the limits you've set to protect your well-being and your values. Here's a road map for getting results when you feel angry.

Turn anger toward a particular outcome, engage your curiosity, reassure yourself, and feel the satisfaction of taking action to successfully protect yourself.

1. ***Verify the situation.*** Before reacting angrily, verify for yourself that you are in fact finding some actual or potential wrong or harm to your well-being. Often, we get angry because something reminds us of a past transgression we suffered. So we get angry defensively to protect ourselves from an imagined transgression, in hopes of avoiding its reoccurrence. Unfortunately, this reaction doesn't work in our favor. We're perceived instead as domineering and difficult to get along with. So, if there is no actual harm as yet, give the situation the benefit of the doubt and remain alert, but curious, as to what will actually happen.

   Tip: If you're feeling angry about a difference with another person in perspective or opinion, ask yourself if you'd rather be right or get the results you're seeking. This one question can save you a lot of unnecessary trouble.

2. ***Take a breath of gratitude.*** If you are actually in harm's way or an injustice has been done to you, take a second to feel grateful that you've seen this danger signal so you can act now to protect yourself. If your anger feels uncontrollable, don't act until you've calmed yourself sufficiently to come up with an effective reaction.

3. ***Define your outcome.*** Before reacting, shift your energy to what you want to accomplish. Define the result you want to achieve from your anger. Do you want someone to stop doing something? Do you want something rectified? Do you want to be sure something never occurs again? Who is the best person to accomplish this? What specific action do you want them to take? Generally, having someone admit he or she is

wrong or getting an apology won't accomplish what you need, although it may make you feel better briefly. What you need is a commitment to correct, stop, or not repeat the harmful action, i.e., covering your costs, making corrections, repairing damage, and so forth.

4. *Get curious.* Use your angry energy to begin exploring ideas for what you can do to elicit a response that will stop, prevent, or rectify any harm to you. Generate possible actions you could take and select the one you believe will be most effective.

5. *Prepare yourself to take action with confidence.* While anger is a powerful feeling, it's sometimes accompanied by a sense of helplessness. Most of us have felt overpowered by authority figures or bullies at times in the past when we were young and could not defend ourselves adequately. Therefore, if you have difficulty believing you can defend yourself successfully, think back to times in the past when you have stopped or prevented yourself from being harmed or wronged, and feel reassured that you can do that again. Acknowledge that it's okay to express your anger and that you can effectively protect yourself with it. Then, imagine yourself taking the action you've identified until you feel satisfied that you've found a solution to the situation and are confident you can carry it out.

6. *Find effective role models.* If you grew up in a family where expressing anger was dangerous, or where you never saw anyone express anger productively, you need some good anger role models. You need to see how someone safely and effectively expresses anger. Look for such people among highly successful individuals who are well respected and admired by those they love and work with. Also, highly effective animal trainers make good anger role models. Such trainers command respect and get results from their animals, with appropriate anger, and they simultaneously convey their affection and respect for the animals even while they're angry at them.

Acting coach and director Gene Bua is one of the most effective people we've met at expressing anger. When Gene is angry about something, you know it. And it's unpleasant. Its cause, however, is always related to something someone failed to do but were fully aware of what he expected of them, because they had agreed to do it. But once he expresses his anger, it's gone. It's been effective and it's over. There's not a trace left. His energy flows right on to the other issues at hand.

For example, all of Gene's acting students sign a contract before their first class that spells out the payment policy. So, when people don't pay their tuition on schedule, as they've agreed to, Gene gets angry. He says something like this in a loud, angry voice: "I expect you to give me your checks at the beginning of the first class of the month! I do my part in this agreement. I'm here every week. I teach the class. I should not have to chase you down to get paid!" And that's that. His message is delivered so powerfully that any late checks are on his chair within minutes, and he's already on to the next matter of business.

Breaking an Anger Habit

Often, people with high standards and high expectations spend a lot of time being angry that life is not as it should be. They are constantly comparing the way things are with the way they think they ought to be, and then feeling angry about the disparity. This, of course, is their right, but an anger habit like this can greatly diminish one's quality of life and the lives of those around them.

To break an anger habit, shift your attention from making negative comparisons to finding similarities between how things should be and how they actually are, and feeling grateful about what you have. Ask yourself what difference it really makes that something isn't exactly as you think it should be. Often, we think things have to go a certain way if we are to obtain our goals, when actually, there are many routes to the same goal, and, amazingly, there is no necessity that they must go any one particular way to achieve your goals.

Highly perfectionistic people are also afraid they won't be able to handle things unless everything goes according to their plans. In such cases, instead of being angry at yourself or the world, build your self-confidence by remembering times when you handled emergencies and unexpected events well so that you can develop a tolerance for the unexpected and respond more easily to whatever happens. As the noted family therapist Virginia Satire was quick to remind us, "Life is not the way it's supposed to be. It's the way it is. The way you cope with it is what makes the difference."

Other issues related to chronic anger when changing directions include:

- Putting up with things you should be confronting until you just can't take anymore and then explode.
- Putting limits on yourself or allowing others to limit what you do so that you are unable to get what you believe you deserve from life.
- Not sufficiently defining what you want and need so that others get the message and respond accordingly.
- Pleasing others from fear of rejection instead of taking care of your own needs. (See **Rejection**)

Depression

Transient depression is an appropriate part of the grieving process and can be expected any time we suffer from a major loss. Thus, depression usually plays some role in the process of changing directions. It's a sign that we need to slow down and withdraw temporarily from the fast-paced responsibilities of life so we can heal a loss. Depression literally slows you down and is the most draining of emotions. When you feel depressed, the past, present, and future all look bleak. Your entire body goes into a withdrawal state. Under such circumstances, it's important to allow yourself to retreat and not try to force yourself into feeling good or keeping up your regular pace.

Depression at times other than a loss, and especially chronic depression, is a very clear signal that you need to change your life in some significant way. It means your life is not providing you with sufficient gratification for you to want to continue it as it is. It tells you that you are pulling away, and the sooner you take action to create better circumstances for yourself, the easier it will be for your depression to move on.

Note: We are not speaking here of clinical depression, which requires medical and/or psychotherapeutic treatment. If depression becomes severe and continues uninterrupted over several weeks, you should seek professional help.

Depression also occurs when:

- You chronically fail to take action to change your existing situation into something more desirable.
- You feel inadequate to face the pressures and conflicts that are preventing you from moving ahead, and you continue instead to endure them rather than doing something to change them. (Also see **Inadequacy** below.)
- You're taking life so personally and seriously that there are little opportunities for joy and laughter.

The solution to all these dilemmas is to recognize how powerless you're feeling and start doing something effective about your situation. But, of course, that's the last thing you feel like doing when you're depressed. When denied our power long enough, we begin to assume nothing can be done to reverse all that we're losing out on in life. So we start to grieve for something we could actually have. Thus, since depression is such a low-energy emotion, the first step in pulling yourself out of it is to generate enough energy to begin taking some action. Here's what we recommend to recharge yourself sufficiently to start moving forward again.

Retreat and assess your situation. Assess whether you've actually suffered a loss. If so, take time to grieve and say goodbye. If not, reflect on the circumstances that have caused you to feel so powerless and resolve to rebuild your energy and confidence so you can change your situation. Then, when you're ready to move on, find some small goodness upon which to build your energy again.

1. ***Find some sweetness.*** Begin by identifying something that is better now than it once was—something in your life you value, treasure, and feel grateful for. It can be anything, even a very small thing, like how you now don't have to drive the long commute your previous job required, that spring is coming and your garden will soon be blooming, or that, despite your problems, you now have the pleasure of wearing a ring your grandmother left you. Don't expect to necessarily start feeling good immediately because you've noticed these things but allow yourself to feel appreciative and grateful for them, even though you aren't feeling great yet.

2. ***Generalize to the future.*** Imagine the simple sweetnesses you've found in your life expanding into other areas in the future. Imagine a future that continues to reflect improvements, even tiny ones, like those you've noticed—a future, for example, of doing something you've never had time to do before, mornings of getting up feeling rested because you aren't dealing with the same pressures you had before, and so forth.

3. ***Find still more sweetness.*** Throughout the day, or at least once at the close of the day, identify the pleasant things in your life, things you're grateful for, things that are even slightly better now. Continue to do this until you have a future in mind that dispels the depression and creates a growing sense of encouragement. This shift will probably not be immediate. But keep using this process. Leslie Cameron-Bandler describes reversing depression as being like lifting a heavy object from the ocean floor: you have to keep pumping more and more bubbles of air into it to get it to rise.

Disappointment

Disappointment is a sign that you need to decide whether you want to carry on toward a particular goal, let it go, or regroup and head off in another direction. It's a frequent visitor when we change directions, but it's the natural response when something we've been hoping for doesn't happen according to plan. Knowing how to manage disappointments, large or small, is a virtual survival skill these days. But, like depression, it's a passive, low-energy emotion, because that's the ideal state for giving up when something's not possible. Here's what you can do when disappointment strikes.

Test out whether there's still a possibility of achieving what you've been hoping for. If not, let go, accept the situation, and allow new feelings of hope to fuel your search for other alternatives for getting what you're seeking. If what you want is still possible, frustration is a far better response than disappointment.

1. ***Apply the possibility test.*** Before giving up hope and succumbing to disappointment, ask yourself if having what you want is still possible through your efforts. To help make this determination, use the following Possibility Test created by Cameron-Bandler and Lebeau:
   - Is there still something you can do to make this happen?
   - Can you think of a time you or anyone else has ever done this?
   - Can you imagine circumstances under which you could do it?
2. ***Accept what cannot be.*** If you discover that what you want is no longer possible (like when Jeanette lost the job as host of her own television show), the disappointment you're feeling, painful as it may be, will help you begin to let go. Tears are appropriate. The tears of grief actually have a different chemical composition than other tears. They are cleansing our bodies so we can move on.
3. ***Allow your energy to move.*** Once you've accepted the impossibility of what you wanted, you'll find that your energy will start to shift and you'll begin to feel hopeful about other ways to meet your needs. You'll begin feeling a desire to pursue other feasible goals.
4. ***Don't give up on what's possible.*** If the Possibility Test indicates that what you want is still possible, then disappointment is not the most productive feeling for you to be having, because it's preparing you to give up.

Once you recognize that what you want is still possible, your emotions will begin to shift. You may feel a glimmer of hope or a renewed sense of resolve or determination. You may also start to feel frustrated that you haven't yet attained your goal. **Frustration** (see below) is an excellent emotion to be feeling in such situations, as it will bring you a flood of fresh energy with which to attack your goals.

Discouragement

Discouragement is the result of taking on such a highly challenging goal that your progress is too slow or nonexistent. The more challenging the new direction you've chosen, the more vulnerable you are to becoming discouraged. Some goals (like becoming an actress, winning an Olympic gold medal, or earning a living doing standup comedy) are, by nature, discouraging, because the odds of success are so low. Unless someone is unusually well prepared, lucky, and well connected, only the most determined and persistent succeed in attaining such lofty goals. Anyone who gets easily discouraged may give up well before they get the chance to attain such levels of success.

To feel *encouraged,* we need to perceive ourselves as making incremental progress toward our goals. If we shoot so high or undertake something so difficult or unclear that we repeatedly fall short of our goals and can sense no progress toward them, we will begin to feel discouraged. In fact, research shows most people begin to feel discouraged whenever they fail to achieve a goal less than 75 percent of the time. So, feeling discouraged is a sign that you need to aim at a target you have a better chance of hitting, something toward which you can feel you're making some headway.

Like the best coaches and trainers, if you don't want to feel discouraged, you need to stop making demands on yourself that are beyond your reach. Instead, you need to help yourself stretch toward your ultimate goals by setting attainable intermediate goals you can meet and continually extend beyond.

In other words, when Ben felt discouraged about the possibility of doing workshops in Italy for writers, the solution was not to give up but to focus instead on something he could reasonably expect to accomplish that would eventually lead toward doing workshops in Italy. Once he set a goal to test his writers' workshop locally, he became excited and encouraged. As we attain smaller achievable goals, we feel increasingly encouraged, and, having met these goals, higher ones become more feasible. Here's how you can shift from feeling discouraged to encouraged.

Feel pride about your existing progress, become curious about what attainable steps you can take next, and start anticipating the results you're seeking . . . until you begin to feel encouraged.

1. **Notice your progress.** Compare where you are now with where you were in the past and note the progress you've made. There may be much you haven't accomplished yet, but focusing on that is how you become discouraged. When the road to starting out in a new direction becomes long and weary, it's easy to miss the progress you've been making, but that's what you need to keep foremost in your mind when you become discouraged.
2. **Compliment yourself.** Focus on whatever progress you've made, no matter how small, and allow yourself to feel a sense of pride in what you have done.
3. **Become curious.** Start wondering what you know you can do next to take you at least one step further.
4. **Remember successes.** Imagine other times in your life when you ultimately achieved challenging goals by taking one step at a time.
5. **See success.** Imagine yourself carrying out your next step successfully until you begin anticipating a positive future and feel encouraged about reaching your ultimate goals.

Failure

Feeling like a failure is actually one of the most basic of human survival tools. Without it, we could never master anything. No one learns to do

Persevering with Confidence

Our willingness to persevere has a great deal to do with whether we motivate ourselves by thinking of what needs to be done as a necessity or as a possibility. How do you feel, for example, when you believe you *have* to do something, *must* do something, *need* to do something, or *should* do something? In other words, when something seems like it is a *necessity*? Check the following choices:

If I think I *have* to do something, do I feel:

- Resistant or determined?
- Guilty or tenacious?
- Desperate or driven?
- Pressured or challenged?
- Overwhelmed or motivated?
- Obligated, regretful, or pleased?

There are no right or wrong answers to these questions. Your answers may even vary, depending on the task or activity involved. But, as you can see, turning a task into a *necessity*, by signing a contract or setting a deadline, versus making it *option*al and leaving it open as to if and when you will do it, can dramatically alter the way you feel about it. The key is knowing what works best for you in various situations. Notice, for example, how you feel when you tell yourself that you *must* do something, as opposed to when you tell yourself you *can* do it. What happens to your emotions when it becomes a choice instead of a requirement? In other words, do you respond better to *possibilities* or *necessities*?

Possibility thinking is often called having a "can-do" attitude. Feelings associated with a can-do attitude include *optimism, caution, curiosity, disappointment, confidence*, and *hope*. But, now, notice how differently you feel if you think something is *impossible* as opposed to *possible*. What happens when someone tells you that you can't do something, or if you shift your focus from what you *can* or *could* do to what you *can't* do?

Some people love the challenge of doing the impossible, but most of us are more likely to feel *helpless, despairing, disappointed, discouraged,* or *inadequate.* In fact, most of us can produce a dramatic shift in the way we feel simply by changing our thoughts from "I *can't* do that" to thinking, "*How* could I do that?" This one simple shift can be a quick way to move from feeling pessimistic to feeling optimistic, from feeling discouraged to feeling encouraged, from feeling disappointed to feeling curious, or from feeling hopeless to feeling motivated.

something perfectly on the first try, other than by accident. As writer James Joyce observed, "Mistakes are the portals of discovery." It's natural to feel like a failure when you've made a mistake or have fallen short of accomplishing a goal. But biologically, this feeling is not intended to be a sign that you should quit or give up, although this is a common misconception people have about this emotion. Rather, feeling like a failure is a sign that you need to do some things differently in the future.

The baby who falls doesn't quit trying to walk. The child who fails to tie his shoe doesn't give up on tying shoes. In fact, think of how quickly and eagerly a young child pushes a parent's helpful hands aside for the chance to try again. Left to run its natural course, the feeling of failure tends to flow naturally into wanting to try again. The desired outcome fuels the drive to keep trying until we succeed. When we fail at something we really want to do, the untethered human brain busily begins calibrating, assimilating, and making thousands of necessary adjustments so we can do better on the next try. Unfortunately, too often, as we grow up, this natural urge to go forward toward completion, which comes from the feeling of failure, gets side-tracked.

At some point, we decide that we are no longer learners. Instead, we start believing that we ought to have mastered certain things and be able to do them successfully, even if many aspects of what we're trying to do are new to us. We decide that if we don't do these things correctly, we've "failed." Failure becomes an end point instead of an intermediary step to success. Based on this attitude, after experiencing multiple failures, we come to equate failure with ruin, and we feel hopeless and defeated, giving up instead of feeling eager and determined to learn what we need to do next. This is the first hurdle you must get over when you start to feel like a failure.

The best way to remain resilient in the face of failure is to have a history of success to fall back on. The parent who takes a child to the swimming pool, for example, and throws him or her into the water before teaching the child to swim is creating a dramatic and memorable failure for that child. We need to be sure we don't do that to ourselves. We need to avoid throwing ourselves into situations without the experience or preparation that would predispose us more to success than failure. You can create ample opportunities for success, for example, by doing your homework on the new direction you're seeking to take. You can be sure you're prepared. Then, occasional failures are just a misstep from which you can quickly recover, learn from, and carry on.

So when you start to feel like a failure, instead of spiraling downward into defeat and despair, take steps that will help you recapture that natural feeling of wanting to jump back in to try again that failure is designed to provide for you. Here's a great way to do this whenever you've made a mistake or failed to accomplish a goal.

Take pride in your efforts, forgive and rectify errors, feel the satisfaction of learning and gaining experience, and use what you've learned to project future success.

1. **Feel pleased with yourself.** You had the courage, fortitude, and confidence to try something new or difficult. People who wait until they're perfect before they act wait forever. Only those who try will ever succeed. So you can and should feel pleased with yourself for having tried.

2. *Forgive yourself.* If your mistakes have caused negative consequences to yourself or others, correct any problems or repair any damage as best you can.

3. *Reassure yourself.* Mistakes and failures are learning opportunities, so you can take pride in learning from your experience. Identify what did and didn't work, and what you will and won't do differently next time. Sometimes, you may not know precisely what went wrong, in which case, resolve to try again as best you can with the intention of discovering more about what you need to do.

4. *Feel satisfied.* There's a certain satisfaction in having acquired new insights and abilities from experience. Feel reassured that, with new insights, you will perform more successfully in the future. Imagine yourself doing so, and instill yourself with a feeling of success.

Fear and Anxiety

Everyone experiences some level of *fear* and *anxiety* when they move out of their comfort zone into the unknown. This is especially true when the stakes are high, as they usually are when you're heading off in a new and unfamiliar direction. Fear and anxiety are normal reactions to an unfamiliar future. They're a sign that you foresee aspects of the future for which you are not prepared that might hold a danger for you. Fear and anxiety are signals that you need to take steps to prepare to cope with or avoid those possible upcoming negative consequences. Thus, trying to ignore your fears is foolhardy. Thank goodness these feelings are alerting you, so you can take needed action now to make sure things go well in the future.

Both fear and anxiety are intense, hyperalert emotions that are designed to incite action to safeguard yourself in the future, even if that future is only a moment away. They both provide such an incredible amount of highly charged energy that you may feel the impulse either to freeze or run. But you can calm your fears by shifting your attention away from the uncertainty of your future to the reality of your present. You can also reduce your fear to a more manageable level by simultaneously taking several deep, relaxing breaths while you concentrate on your present situation.

Here's a step-by-step process you can use to walk yourself through a fear attack.

Focus on the safety of the present, become curious about what you can do to prevent the negative things you fear, review past successful experiences you handled until you begin to feel confident you can handle this one, too, and anticipate taking the action you need to take to avoid what you fear.

1. ***Be here now.*** Quickly bring your attention into the present. Since fear signals a possible future danger, when you start to feel anxious, immediately shift your attention away from the dreaded future to the present and concentrate on where you are in the here and now. That's the only place from which you can take action anyway, so it's the best place to be when you feel apprehensive.

2. ***Note that you're safe for the moment.*** For example, if you are feeling anxious about an upcoming call you must make, stop thinking for the time being about that call and recognize that, right now, you're just fine.

3. ***Focus on what you can do now.*** Concentrate on how you could protect yourself from the possible negative outcomes you fear until you begin feeling safe in the moment. Click into your curiosity. How could you prepare yourself to handle the future situation you're imagining? What are you afraid will happen? How could you prevent that? Become intrigued and fascinated with finding the answers to these questions.

    Begin breaking down what you can do into small, specific steps. For example, if you're going on an interview for a dream job, how can you make sure you're sufficiently well prepared to make a winning impression? If you're anxious about having enough income coming in next month when your sideline business goes full-time, what steps can you take now to line up enough business in order to feel secure? If you are afraid you won't meet an important deadline, what steps can you take now to avoid having that problem?

4. ***Remember success.*** Confidence is the antidote to fear, says sports psychologist Alexander Roman, so recall times in the past when you prepared yourself to successfully avoid things you feared until you begin to

feel a sense of your own capability. Other than for the purpose of identifying what you can do to prepare now, avoid repeatedly recalling the times when you were not prepared.

5. *Imagine successfully protecting yourself.* See yourself preparing to meet the challenge or threat you anticipate. Mentally rehearse the steps you will take to prepare until you feel confident in your ability to avoid what you fear and achieve positive results in the future.

6. *Anticipate success.* Begin anticipating the experience of success that you've been rehearsing. As you anticipate meeting the challenge, you may even begin looking forward to doing it.

Tip: Anxiety produces an intense energy that's designed for taking action. The dictionary definitions of anxiety reflect its two-sided role. First, it's defined as "an uneasiness of the mind caused by a concern for the future." But its second definition is "eager earnestness or intense desire." This two-sided aspect of anxiety means that if we don't use this intense emotion to act on our concerns, it turns inward and builds up, and we begin to feel like we're under a lot of pressure. If we still fail to take action, we soon feel as if we're living in a pressure cooker. (Also see **Rejection, Failure,** *and* **Self-Doubt,** *as aspects of performance anxiety.)*

Frustration

While most people don't like to feel frustrated, it's actually a useful emotion in situations that require continued effort and determination. Unlike disappointment and depression, which drain our energy and slow us down, frustration provides a surge of intense energy that propels us to action. Here's how to put frustration to work for you.

Welcome the energy that frustration provides, focus on your outcome, and encourage yourself to persevere with reminders of past successful efforts.

1. *Welcome frustration.* Without frustration, we just might run out of energy and give up. Frustration is a motivator. It's like sitting on a hot stove; it gets us moving.

Other Tips for Overcoming Fears

Here are several ways workshop participants tell us how they deal with fear and anxiety:

- "I remind myself that courage comes later, after the fact, and to go ahead and do what I need to do."
- "I write down how I would like to be thinking about the situation. Then I write down all the negative reactions I have for why I can't feel that way until I understand them and can change my feelings."
- "I feel the fear and do it anyway."
- "I believe that what you resist persists, so I don't try to avoid my fears; I look at them and then I can decide what to do about them."
- "I ask myself, has that ever happened?"
- "I ask myself if I'm amplifying what might happen and then ask myself instead what would probably really happen."

2. *Focus on your outcome.* Take a deep breath and focus on the fact that what you want is still possible. Feel how much you want it. Is it still a 7 or above? Up to a point, the more frustrated you are, the more motivated you're likely to be. If you didn't care, you wouldn't try. Of course, when frustration becomes too intense we feel overwhelmed, so then we need to simplify and clarify our situation to reduce our frustration to a manageable level. (See **Overwhelming Feelings** below.)

3. *Remember past successes.* Recall times in the past when it didn't look like you could make the changes you wanted in your life, but through your continued efforts you ultimately did get what you wanted. This will help you turn your frustrations into an "I-can" mindset.

4. *Be patient yet determined.* Impatience often originates in doubt and fear. But if you keep imagining the desired outcome you know is still possible to be attained, impatience recedes, and in its place you can begin feeling a renewed sense of enthusiasm and excitement, as you start

anticipating the outcome you're seeking. As you start looking forward to enjoying your designed outcome, you'll find it's much easier to persevere.

Tip: Impatience is always a fast-paced, high-energy emotion. It can stir us to action or simply intensify our frustration. Use it to get yourself and others moving, but when things cannot go any faster, replace it with anticipation of eventual success.

Guild

*G*uilt is a much-maligned emotion, because it can spiral downward into feelings of worthlessness, hopelessness, and despair. Actually, though, guilt can be a very helpful emotion. It's a sign that you have violated one of your own personal standards. It informs you that you've let yourself down, that you haven't lived up to what you expect of yourself, and it provides you with the opportunity to take steps to ensure that you won't violate that standard again.

In fact, a study by Case Western Reserve University psychologist Roy F. Baumeister found that, while people will often try to rationalize their guilt, attending to it can be good for both you and any others involved. Guilt means you're feeling *empathy* for someone you've wronged, or are *anxious* about losing a relationship you value or being rejected or excluded by others because of your behavior. The discomfort of feeling guilty serves as a motivator to correct or make up for your behavior.

So, if you are sufficiently tolerant of your own imperfections, as any good coach or mentor would be, you need not feel worthless when you haven't lived up to something you expect of yourself. You can look honestly at yourself without spiraling downward and take steps for doing better in the future. Here's one road map for dealing with guilt.

Tip: The feeling of guilt can be complicated by the fact that sometimes it arises when we're trying to live up to someone else's standards or expectations instead of our own. For example, a woman might feel guilty about working late because her parents told her her family should always come first. So, guilt also provides an opportunity for us to clarify what we believe and value.

1. ***Have you, in fact, violated your own standards?*** Or are you are feeling guilty because you haven't done what someone else thought you should do? If you are feeling guilty because you are trying to meet someone else's expectations and have failed, identify what your own standards are in this situation and act accordingly. If you haven't actually broken your own standards, you probably won't feel guilty any longer, and, once you realize this, you can clarify with others what they can and cannot expect from you if necessary.

2. ***Get curious.*** If you have violated your own standards or expectations, begin with a sense of curiosity to evaluate whether this is a standard that you still want to maintain. If it is, respect and fully appreciation and acknowledge that you want to make sure you won't violate this standard again.

3. ***Think back.*** Recall times in the past when you successfully lived up to your standards, even though it was difficult, and feel reassured about your ability to live up to your personal standards now.

4. ***Create a plan.*** Imagine yourself taking the necessary steps to live up to your standards in the most difficult of situations and feel pleased and confident about your ability to do so.

Hopelessness

Feelings often occur on a continuum, from small to large or from weak and mild to strong and intense. Disappointment, for example, is mild in comparison to hopelessness. Yet hopelessness is milder than depression. These three emotions are similar in that they all involve the prospect of a future without something we desire. They are all low-energy emotions that prepare us to let go of something of value that we've lost.

Hopelessness, however, is more final than disappointment but not as bleak as depression. It's the appropriate emotion to feel when you've done everything you can do but it isn't enough. It comes up when you can't envision a future that includes something you've wanted and is designed to prepare you for giving up any expectation of attaining it in the future.

Therefore, the first thing you need to do when you feel hopeless is to ask yourself if, in fact, there is nothing else you can do. Is there any possibility you can still do something to achieve what you're seeking? If there is, imagine the future you want and allow yourself to feel the *frustration* of not yet having accomplished it. Feel challenged and determined to discover what remains to be done and to do it. As Alexander Pope penned, "Hope springs eternal in the human breast."

If you've done all there is to do, however, it's time to heed your feeling of hopelessness and let go. You can help yourself to let go by doing the following.

Feel reassured by past times when giving up on or losing something of value, albeit painful, led to something else of value, and accept that you must now move on.

1. *Remember greener pastures.* Remember times in your life when you let go of having something you wanted and discovered other things that were equally or even more satisfying.
2. *Take comfort.* Feel reassured by these memories, accept what cannot be attained, but open yourself to the possibility of discovering something new or better.
3. *Move on.* Imagine yourself in the future, walking away from the goal you've wanted and moving on with confidence toward something else that you can accomplish.

Breakthrough: Susan and Peter

When Susan and Peter left the public-relations firm they were working at when they met and married, they were excited about their plans for launching a nationwide seminar program that would help couples rebuild shaky relationships. They prepared brochures, took out ads in the paper, created lots of media exposure for their inaugural seminar, and held a small but successful first seminar.

Unfortunately, the expenses of holding the seminar exceeded the money they brought in. There was no money left for promoting a second one. Still hopeful, however, they used telemarketing—working the phones themselves until they finally filled another seminar. It, too, was a success for those who attended, but again, expenses still exceeded income.

After several months, Susan and Peter were exhausted and on the verge of bankruptcy. As weeks passed, their dream of a national seminar looked increasingly hopeless. They had done everything they could think of. And although it was painful, they decided to let go of that dream before it did them in. Once they accepted that their future would not include conducting their couples' seminars across the nation, they were free to begin thinking of what else they could do. Since they were both highly skilled public-relations specialists, they decided they would open their own public-relations firm, doing publicity for seminar leaders.

By shifting their focus to the history of success they'd had in PR, they began envisioning a new future, one in which they were running a successful firm and were able to proceed toward that goal with confidence. Their subsequent success in PR provided them with the funds to conduct, through their church, free seminars for dysfunctional families. Susan now says, "This work is actually more gratifying than the original seminars we'd planned. When everything seemed so hopeless, it was actually just a sign that we needed to proceed in a different direction."

Inadequacy

Inadequacy is designed to take you out of a situation before you get in over your head and to give yourself a chance to become better prepared. It usually results from comparing what we can do, or have done, with what someone else can do, has done, or thinks we should do. It's a passive emotion that tends to stop us in our tracks, but it can be invaluable when we're truly not prepared to make the change we're about to attempt. Feeling inadequate gives us a chance to slow down, assess our level of preparedness, and take the time to expand our skills and abilities.

Studies show, though, that often the people who are the most inadequate don't recognize it. They think they're perfectly competent and can't understand why they have such bad luck in life. To understand their poor results, they need to start comparing what they're doing, or not doing, with what people do who have successfully made the changes they're wanting to make.

Unfortunately, many high achievers who are quite adequate don't use this emotional tool effectively, either. They feel inadequate, even when they're perfectly competent and thoroughly prepared. They make a habit of comparing themselves with very successful people because they aspire to similar levels of achievement. But in making comparisons, they focus on the ways in which they fall short, not on ways they could improve. The result is a chronic feeling of inadequacy, and, of course, we don't perform at our best when we're feeling inadequate, so their beliefs become a self-fulfilling prophecy. Another common consequence of this misuse of inadequacy is to limit your dreams and think small instead of going for what you really want.

Here are some steps you can take whenever you start to feel inadequate:

Connect with capability and competence, build confidence, proceed from strength, compare to success, and build capability.

1. *Remind yourself of your strengths.* Focus your attention on what you know you can do and have done well. Review your strengths in detail— your capabilities, accomplishments, and past demonstrations of competence.
2. *Regain confidence.* Continue reviewing your strengths and assets until you begin to feel adequate to do those things you know you can do well.
3. *Assess the situation from strength.* When you're feeling adequate again, compare your many assets with those who have attained the success you're seeking, and identify possible areas you might want to improve on

or be better prepared for. Take whatever action is appropriate from a sense of your own competency.

If you make a habit of comparing yourself negatively to people whose success or skills you admire, here's what you can do.

4. ***Pick the right role models.*** Make sure those you choose as role models are people you actually want to be like. If you tend to aspire to be like someone whom other people think you should be like, you are doomed to feel inadequate. An intellectual sister who is always comparing her success to that of her athletic brother, for example, is setting herself up to feel inadequate no matter how well she performs academically. The brother has a completely different set of skills and abilities than hers, and she has no desire to acquire them. You'll never feel adequate if you're comparing yourself to someone who is inherently different from the person you are or want to become. So look for people to admire who are sufficiently like the person you are at heart and aspire to become.

5. ***Compare yourself positively.*** Instead of noticing the ways you don't measure up to those you admire, notice the ways in which you are similar. Even if you find this hard to do at first, search until you find similarities. You will. We only truly admire people who reflect an image of what we already know is the best in ourselves. So we have to train our eyes to see what's similar.

6. ***Use their achievements to set your goals.*** Do acknowledge differences that explain why your role models have excelled to the level you aspire to, i.e., having fifteen years more experience or having studied extensively in related fields. It's useless to expect that you should have attained levels of mastery on which they have spent many more years than you to acquire. But you can gain from observing the results of their efforts and learn from them by doing those things you admire in them. When you see or hear them doing what you admire, say to yourself, "That's for me!" "That's what I'm going to do!" "That's how I'm going to be!"

7. ***Imagine yourself doing what you admire.*** As you watch your role models at work, imagine yourself inside their skin, doing what they're doing. How does it feel to be them? Then imagine how you would do it. How would you integrate your own skills, values, and personality into what

Confidence Builders

Here are a few things you can do when you need to boost your self-confidence:

- Adjust your posture to reflect confidence. Stand up tall and straight. Shoulders back, chest forward. Look straight ahead. Make eye contact. Speak up. Walk with a commanding stride.
- Remember times when you felt and acted confident.
- Compliment yourself on what you do well. Remind yourself of things you admire about yourself.
- See yourself doing something amazing, such as climbing a mountain or flying a plane.
- Identify something in your current situation that you are already handling with confidence.
- Feel your own backbone, and imagine it to be a steel rod.
- Identify a clear outcome for yourself in the situation.
- Play a particularly affecting piece of music in your head, one that makes you feel confident.
- Think of people who make you feel confident and imagine them small enough to be able to sit on your shoulder and whisper encouraging messages into your ear.

Reprinted with permission from The Emotional Hostage *by Leslie Cameron-Bandler and Michael Lebeau (Futurepace.)*

they're doing? As you imagine yourself in their shoes, you should quickly get a sense of what you're already well prepared to do and what you aren't. You may discover you're ready to go to it or realize there are several areas you want to be better prepared in.

8. *Set goals.* Resolve to learn how to do the things you aspire to do. Take action to master skills and carry out the tasks you need to build your

mastery. Read books, take classes, do trial runs and gain as much experience as you can.

9. *Act as if.* In the course of your day, act to the extent that you can, as if you've already achieved the mastery of your role models. Apply what you've been learning. Notice how this colors the way you walk, talk, and perform.

Irresponsibility

Irresponsibility is one of those feelings that our society holds in contempt. Sometimes, if we don't live up to our own demands, we begin accusing ourselves of being irresponsible, which leads to feeling guilty, ashamed, angry, or resentful. Actually, feeling irresponsible is a signal that one of the following is true:

- You don't believe anything needs to be done.
- You don't think it's your job to do.
- You don't believe you are capable of doing it.

If you determine that something needs to be done and that there's no one better qualified or situated than you to do it, you will probably begin feeling responsible and start considering how you will go about doing it. So, when you start feeling irresponsible, give the situation this "Responsibility Test" by Cameron-Bandler and Lebeau:

- Does something need to be done?
- Are you the most qualified person to do it?
- Are you able to do it?

If you agree that something needs to be done and you're the person to do it but feel you can't, you will probably start to feel inadequate. In that case, you will want to develop the ability and confidence you need to carry out your responsibilities. (Also see INADEQUACY.) If you don't think anything needs to be done or that you're not the one to do it, make this known to anyone else involved, so they can make other arrangements instead of counting on you.

Lethargy

Lethargy is an emotion you feel when faced with tasks you know need to be done but don't want to do and therefore lack the necessary will or motivation to carry them out. It's a passive, slow, low-energy feeling that signals disinterest or lack of involvement in what you feel needs to be done. It's a sign you either need to:

1. Accept that you don't want to do what's involved in making a particular change and make other plans.
2. Figure out how you can make the tasks at hand sufficiently desirable that you are willing to put the energy into doing them.

If you want to proceed in the direction you've chosen, heed the signal lethargy is sending and take the following steps:

Let your curiosity motivate you to become determined and feel the ambition to do what's needed.

1. *Review the value.* Is what's making you feel so lethargic worth doing? Is it important to achieving your goals? If the tasks at hand aren't worthwhile, why are you expecting yourself to do them? Let yourself off the hook. You'll be amazed at how quickly your energy and your emotions will shift.
2. *Find some shred of interest.* If the tasks are worthwhile, ask what aspects of what you need to do might have at least some mild interest for you. Begin asking yourself questions about what's involved, questions that have some importance to you.
3. *Pick up your tempo.* As you question what's involved, pick up your energy—even if that means doing something like playing some moderately paced music in the background while you work or rubbing your hands together vigorously.

Other Tips for Staying Energized

Here are a few of the things our workshop participants do to avoid lethargy:

- "I believe energy is a decision. Instead of talking about how tired I am, I talk about how energized I am."
- "I look forward to tiny boosters, like having something for lunch that I really like or relishing little accomplishments and celebrating little victories."
- "Doing something differently energizes me, like taking a different route to work."
- "Taking a break to walk the dog helps pick up my energy level."
- "Staying out of other people's problems is one of the best ways I keep my energy level up."
- "I stay out of bragging competitions about how tough my work is and how hard I'm overworking."

4. *Pique your curiosity.* As you ask about the tasks at hand, you'll probably begin to feel curious about your answers. Shift that feeling of wanting to know the answers to feeling that you must know the answers, and you'll start to feel motivated and determined to find them.
5. *Think about what interests you.* Finding what interests you about these tasks will help you to begin feeling more ambitious, and, assuming you've had enough sleep and R&R, you'll start to feel motivated to begin doing the most worthwhile of the things you need to do.

Overwhelming Feelings

Feeling *overwhelmed* is a signal that you're trying to take care of too much too soon. You have too many things to do all at once and haven't been setting priorities. You're undoubtedly acutely aware of many things you must do immediately, but since you can't do them all simultaneously, your mind and body are racing from one thing to another, trying to do some of everything, accomplishing little of anything.

As you rush around like a whirl of energy that doesn't know where to land, the pressure builds, and eventually your overwhelming feelings spiral downward into feeling immobilized and hopeless. But, if you focus and utilize the maelstrom of energy that being overwhelmed provides, before it spirals downward, you can use it to accomplish a lot. Here's how you can use this tool effectively when you first start to feel overwhelmed.

Slow down, break what needs doing into smaller pieces, set priorities, and focus on one thing at a time.

1. *Slow down.* Take a long, deep, relaxing breath.
2. *Create a mental space.* Remind yourself you have all the time in the world, even if it doesn't feel like you do. You have control over the use of your time. It doesn't control you.
3. *Break it up.* Look at what needs to be done and break down the overwhelming situation into various smaller tasks. Create a list. Don't panic when you see how long it is. Start setting priorities. What needs to be done first, second, and so on? What doesn't need doing at all or, at least, not right now? Who's saying it all has to be done immediately? How are you pressuring yourself?
4. *Switch your thinking.* Once you've broken what needs to be done into manageable pieces, stop thinking "I must do this," and tell yourself, as you work at a sensible pace, "I can do this."
5. *Buy time if necessary.* If there is actually more to do than can be done, make plans to round up some help or get extensions on expected deadlines.
6. *Focus on the one task that must be done first.* After having taken the above steps, you'll probably be feeling motivated to begin the first task and capable of moving on to the next one once that's completed. So start working on the one thing that needs to be done first. Then go to the next, and the next.

Sometimes, as your sense of control returns, you may realize that you

> ### Other Tips for Dealing with Overwhelming Feelings
>
> Here are several things our workshop participants do when they feel overwhelmed:
>
> - "I remember how my mother was always overwhelmed by life, and I recognize that this feeling is more her way of handling life than mine."
> - "I take time out to play basketball. This frees my mind and gives me perspective to see solutions."
> - "I ask myself 'Is it good enough?' and remind myself good enough is good enough."
> - "I take a break and do some strenuous physical exercise."
> - "I purposely do something imperfectly to keep myself from being so demanding."
> - "I go horseback riding and just go wherever the horse wants to go until I'm relaxed and my mind is clear."

need to drop, reschedule, delegate, or otherwise engage others to help you carry out certain aspects of your commitments.

Rejection

Whether it's being turned down for a home loan by one bank after another, losing out on another job interview, being passed over for a desired contract, or having a home buyer turn their nose up at your house when you put it on the market, changing directions usually means coming face-to-face with rejection. No one likes it, but we all have to deal with it. The purpose of rejection, of course, is to rid our lives of things that are harmful or no longer useful to us, and it's important for us to be able to reject that which isn't consistent with what we want in life. Rejection is the opposite of something we all enjoy: appreciation.

If we've been rejected in the past by people who were important to us, like or parents or schoolmates, we may have become hypersensitive to being rejected and conclude that our efforts generally won't be appreciated by others. Thus, we develop another hybrid fear—the fear of rejection, which causes us to do what we think will please others instead of what will please us. But, of course, we're rarely at our best when trying to be what someone else wants instead of who we are and, thus, by trying to avoid rejection we set up the potential for the very thing we fear. But here are a series of questions you can use when the pain of rejection begins nipping at your heels. In fact, as a rule of thumb, the more difficulty you have rejecting things that aren't what you want or need, the more likely you are to have problems with being rejected.

1. *Do you still want to pursue the new direction you've been seeking to take?* When faced with repeated rejection, it's tempting to conclude, "Hey, I don't need this!" or "Who needs to put up with this?" And, of course, that's absolutely right. You don't have to put up with situations where you're consistently unappreciated. You have choices. You don't have to head in a particular direction. Sometimes, once you start pursuing a direction, however, you discover there are aspects of it that dampen your interest. So, you need to feel free to choose another direction at any point along the way. But is that what you want? Or do you still want to proceed?

2. *Ask yourself how much do you want to do this?* You may still want to proceed, but how much do you want go in this new direction? Do you want it enough to put up with whatever it takes for as long as it takes? The more rejection a particular change involves, the more you need to want it. Are you still at a 7 or above on a 10-point scale? If so, why let one person, or even a series of people, stop you?

3. *Are you taking this too personally?* Like artists, when we're designing our lives, it's easy to overidentify with what we're trying to create. There's a tendency to think the bank or the buyer is rejecting you and judging you personally as inadequate. In actuality, most rejections have less to do with you but instead with the circumstances of the persons involved. They're simply doing what's best for them. As Laura Huxley put it so

nicely, "You are not the target." It's important to stay sufficiently detached to realize it's usually not even about you. Truth is, you don't want anyone or anything that doesn't want you. The more aware you are of this, the more likely you are to ascertain just what your circumstances are and what you need to do to find a milieu where you're appreciated.

4. *Is that "no" really a "no"?* Before becoming impaled on the claws of rejection, consider that a "no" is not necessarily a "no." While we're growing up, parents and teachers tell us, "When I say no, I mean no. And I don't want to hear another word out of you." So, most of us learn to take "no" seriously. But, in the grown-up world, "no" isn't necessarily so. Many people routinely say "no," at first, simply to determine if the person is serious enough to pursue the issue. And many people change their mind sometime after talking with you. Times change. Circumstances change. We need to hear "no" as meaning "not now."

5. *Who's the best judge?* No one is in a better position than you to appreciate your value. To feel bad about someone rejecting what you're offering or proposing is to allow someone else to determine your value. If the reactions you're getting suggest that there's room for improvement, welcome the feedback and make the needed changes so you can harvest the rewards of your true value. Then, go back to those whose support you need and show them what you've got.

6. *What can you celebrate right now?* It can be hard to keep moving ahead when you encounter rejection after rejection. Success is a journey, and we need to see progress. We need to experience some rewards to keep going. If you wait to celebrate until you arrive at your destination, you may give up before you get there. So, celebrate each milestone along the way. This will provide you with the recognition and appreciation you need to keep going, even in the face of rejection. The more you appreciate yourself, the more likely others will appreciate you, too.

7. *Who thinks you're great?* One of the best antidotes to fear of rejection is a little appreciation from your friends. When you're feeling your worst, ask yourself, "Who thinks I'm great? Who always believes in me?" Get in touch with these folks fast. Also, whenever you receive thank-you letters or other notes of appreciation, save them. Put them in a "stroke

file." At times when you're getting a lot of no's, get out those notes and remind yourself there are people who value and appreciate you so much that they were moved to be sure you knew about it.

8. *How can you take matters into your own hands?* Nothing can finish off any endeavor more effectively than having to wait endlessly for someone else's okay to get under way. Entertainers often face this type of chronic rejection. They can't get a part until they're in the union, and they can't get in the union until they get a part. The successful ones don't wait for someone to discover them. They find some way to perform. They may, for instance, volunteer to appear in trade films or organize their own theater group.

So don't let your success rest in the hands of someone else. Don't wait for another no. If the bank won't give you the loan you need to expand, raise your own funds. If you can't seem to get a bid, volunteer to do a project for someone who could influence future customers.

Remember, success is always attracted to bright and shiny moving targets. So if you're not getting the breaks you need, rather than feeling rejected, take charge and make your own breaks.

Self-Doubt

In changing directions, we're pressured by the demands of juggling both the life we've been leading and the new life we're trying to put on the road. Yet, we must rise to the occasion and perform under that pressure. The pressure to perform on demand produces the common hybrid of anxiety known as *performance anxiety*. It's the opposite of what we all hope for, the confidence to perform well under pressure. Usually, performance anxiety is a by-product of *self-doubt*, a concern about our ability to do what's required to accomplish our goals that leaves us fearful about the future. The source of that fear is not a real and present danger, however. It's the result of our own perception of what we may or may not be able to do and the repercussions that we imagine could follow.

The best cure for performance anxiety is mastery. Once you know you can handle anything that might come along, anxiety about doing it usually goes away. There's nothing like experience to take off the pressure, so if performance anxiety hits you, begin by identifying what you know you can do. Then, challenge yourself to go one step beyond that and prepare as follows for doing well.

1. ***Build a history of success.*** Rehearse or try out what you're wanting to do until you know you can consistently do it well. Start with smaller projects, for example, until you have a string of positive memories of successfully doing whatever is required to succeed. When interviewed on A&E, the lyricist and composer Stephan Sondheim explained that when he wanted to do his own Broadway musical, his mentor told him to do the following:

   1. Produce an existing musical that has already been successful.
   2. Then, try taking a successful play you like and musicalize it.
   3. Then, take a flawed play and musicalize that.
   4. Next, select a work that wasn't written as a play and musicalize that.
   5. Finally, after you've done that, you'll be ready to create and produce your own original musical.

   Carefully building such a sequential track record of success is invaluable. It predisposes you to succeed each step along the way while you're building experience to perform at an even higher level. If you can't actually do run-throughs of what you want to do, you can at least mentally rehearse your actions repeatedly. Peak performance expert Charles Garfield found that mental rehearsal is one of the key strategies used by world-class athletes to achieve their best performances.

   As Eleanor Roosevelt said, "I believe anyone can conquer fear by doing the things he fears to do, provided he keeps doing them until he gets a record of successful experiences behind him."

2. ***Get the bugs out of whatever you need to do well.*** Do a series of dry runs where mistakes don't matter. An Olympic athlete wouldn't go into competition with a new routine he or she had never performed well in

practice. A concert pianist would never go on stage to play a piece he'd never rehearsed. Confidence goes up and anxiety comes down with each successful experience you have.

3. *Mentally replay positive memory strings.* When you need to perform at your best under pressure, mentally review your track record of success many times. Whenever doubts creep in, remind yourself that you've done what you will be doing before, and therefore you can do it again. Positive memory strings provide ample evidence that you can succeed.

4. *Convince yourself you'll do well.* The more convinced you are that you'll do well, the more confident you'll feel, and your anxiety will disappear. To convince yourself of your capability, think of several things you know you can do well. Perhaps you're a good driver or a good tennis player. Then, ask yourself how you know that you'll do a good job with these tasks and how many times it took you to demonstrate this to yourself before you were convinced. This is your "convincer" strategy. We each have one. Once you know yours, you can use it to convince yourself of your ability to carry out any task well. Once you are convinced, you'll not only perform well, but everyone else is likely to be convinced as well. If you believe this, so will others.

Other Tips on Handling Self-Doubt

Here are several things our workshop participants do to handle feelings of self-doubt:

- "I realize I'm comparing myself to what others are expecting, and instead I focus on what I expect of myself."
- "When I feel like I'm on shaky ground, I imagine myself standing on solid ground."
- "I imagine myself owning the room, and I arrange things they way I feel most comfortable—if not literally, then mentally."
- "I realize I'm feeling small, like a child, and shift my self-image to seeing myself as the large adult I am."

5. ***Remember: fear, anxiety, and excitement feel very similar.*** These emotions all provide a high state of energy, which is one of the cornerstones of peak performance. So turn your anxiety into excitement. Instead of acting on the impulse you feel to run away, use that energy to run headlong toward what you want. Let the energy you feel flow through you into your performance. It's safe to feel so supercharged, so don't sit on your energy or try to contain it. Use it and it will empower you.

Stuck

Feeling *stuck* is a sign that you need to step away from whatever approach you're using and find another one. Feeling stuck is a way of telling yourself that you've got to do something differently. It's a passive but high-energy emotion. Therefore, taking any action will usually help get you moving again. Here's what you can do when you feel stuck.

Appreciate all the energy you have that's going nowhere. Use it to become curious about what you could do differently. Reassure yourself you can and proceed with confidence.

1. ***Appreciate all the bound-up energy you're feeling.*** Start using that energy to get curious about various other ways you could proceed. Just seeing new possibilities will help you move out of your passivity.
2. ***Call on your track record.*** Think back to other times in your life when you felt stuck but were able to come up with new options that worked out well for you. Do this until you feel reassured about coming up with options for this situation. Imagine yourself generating new options for this situation until you feel confident about finding a new course of action.
3. ***Generate at least ten options.*** No matter how outrageous your ideas might seem, think of other things you could do to make progress toward your goals. Include the possibility that you could even change or reverse your goals.
4. ***Select one.*** Choose something to try out, the one option you like most, a specific action you can take now and do it.

Avoiding Misperceptions That
Will Trip You Up

Our feelings are based on our perception of our situation. If our perceptions are faulty, the emotions that rush forward to assist us will be inappropriate for the situation. They not only won't help us, but they'll probably further complicate whatever we're dealing with. Here are four common ways we make misperceptions and how we can avoid them.

OVERGENERALIZATION

Because something, or someone, has been one way in the past, you may assume that it will be that way now. You may generalize that what happened in one or more situations in the past is happening, or will happen again, in your current situation. If your parents got angry, for example, when you asserted yourself, you may overgeneralize to assume that everyone is trying to keep you from expressing and asserting yourself. The ensuing anger you felt toward others will not be helpful, since most people won't understand why you were angry. Some might even get angry in response to your anger.

To avoid overgeneralizing, ask yourself how this situation is the same and how it is different from previous situations. How have you changed? How has the situation changed? How might others involved have changed?

PROJECTION

Because you feel or think a certain way, you may assume that others in the situation think and feel that way, too. If you are aware, for example, that you left material out of a presentation and are therefore critical of yourself, you may project that others in the room are also critical, when, in fact, they have no knowledge of what you've left out and so are not at all critical. Or sometimes, because something has been one way in the past, we project that it will be that way again.

To avoid projecting, look for concrete signs of the conclusions you reach. If someone is scowling or using a cross tone of voice, for example, verify that you're reading the situation correctly by checking out the accuracy of your observations, i.e., "Do you disagree? Are you disappointed?"

DISTORTION

If we have incomplete information, we tend to fill in the missing pieces and imagine what seems to be a likely scenario. Sometimes, these assumptions distort the actual situation. Or, if we don't like what we're hearing, we may imagine it more positively or automatically fear the worst. For example, if you don't hear back from someone you called, you might conclude that they aren't interested in a proposal you've made, when, in fact, they're simply behind schedule.

To avoid distortions, try imagining a variety of possibilities and test your assumptions by seeking additional information.

DISCOUNTING

Sometimes, we ignore key information about a situation because we don't want to face it, find it irrelevant or improbable, or don't think it's important. So we fail to notice it, or, if we do notice it, we decide it's not significant. For example, if you assume your project is on track even though you haven't received your last two progress payments, you could be discounting a major problem in the making.

To avoid discounting, think about the situations you approach from various perspectives: your own, that of the others involved, the history behind the situation, and the future implications of the situation. This will help you account for all the important variables, so you can operate from a realistic but confident premise.

By avoiding misperceptions, you can get a more accurate picture of what's going on in your life, and your emotions—from glad to sad and mad to scared—will be available to guide you to do the right thing at the right time in order to head off in a new direction!

References

Cameron-Bandler, Leslie, and Michael Lebeau. *The Emotional Hostage: Rescuing Your Emotional Life.* Futurepace. ISBN 0-93257-303-7.

Chopra, Deepak. *Unconditional Life: Mastering the Forces that Shape Personal Reality.* Bantam Books. ISBN 0-553-07609-4.

Garfield, Charles A. *Peak Performance: The Mental Techniques of the World's Greatest Athletes.* Tarcher/Putnam. ISBN 0-87477-214-1.

Goleman, Daniel. *Emotional Intelligence.* Bantam Books. ISBN 0-553-09503-X.

Orstein, Robert. *The Evolution of Consciousness: The Origins of the Way We Think.* Touchstone Books. ISBN 0-67179-224-5.

Other Resources

BOOKS

The Complete Idiot's Guide to Changing Careers. Charland, William. MacMillan. ISBN 0-028-61977-3. Not just job changing but career changing is Charland's forte.

Country Bound! Ross, Marilyn, and Tom Ross. Upstart Publishing Company. ISBN 1-574-10069-6. Advocates of trading urban for country lifestyle, the Rosses tell how.

Executive in Passage. Marrs, Donald. Barrington Sky Publishing. ISBN 0-925-88787-9. In sharing his own inspirational story, Marrs deals not only with material success but also the issues of meaning and fulfillment.

Finding Your Perfect Work: The New Career Guide to Making a Living, Creating a Life. Edwards, Paul, and Sarah. Tarcher/Putnam. ISBN 0-87477-795-X. How to match your desires with your talents to find a career that will support the life you want to live.

Man With No Name: Turning Lemons into Lemonade. Amos, Wally and Denton, Camilla. Aslan Publishing. ISBN 0-94403-157-9. Inspiring and heartfelt evidence of how change can be a positive force in our lives even when it's unexpected.

Managing Transitions. Bridges, William. Perseus Press. ISBN 0-201-55073-3. Bridges is the author of a number of helpful books for those engaged in career change.

The Practical Dreamer's Handbook. Edwards, Paul, and Sarah Edwards. Tarcher/Putnam. ISBN 1-585-42055-7. In this book we reject both the traditional notion of working for decades so that you can retire and then do what you want, as well as the popular model of setting goals and engaging in minute-by-minute planning. Instead we provide a blueprint for combining imagination with practicality.

Rites of Passage at $100,000 to $1 Million+. Lucht, John. Henry Holt & Company, Inc. ISBN 0-942-78530-4. Focuses on employment.

The 7 Levels of Change. Smith, Rolf. Summit Publishing Group. ISBN 1-565-30207-9. Offers tools usable both personally and in organizations.

Taking Charge of Change. Smith, Douglas K. Perseus Press. ISBN 0-201-91604-5. Managers in organizations can benefit from the diagnostic tools in this book and advice on implementing change.

Who Moved My Cheese. Johnson, Spenser. Putnam Publishing Group. ISBN 0-399-14446-3. The inspirational little book that may have prepared you for *Changing Directions Without Losing Your Way.*

WEB SITES

www.changingcourse.com—The web site of Valerie Young, who now publishes an ezine version of her Changing Course Newsletter, in which she deals with life change of which career change is a part.

www.simplegoodlife.com—Resources, advice, support, and information for how to have the time for what you love, for what you love with those you love in a place, at a pace, and for a price you can afford. Would you guess—our web site?

Index

About the Authors

Paul & Sarah Edwards are the authors of fourteen books about how to live the life you want to live. Their home office is in Pine Mountain, California, where they operate the Pine Mountain Institute, which sponsors their web site, www.simplegoodlife.com, their weekly show on BusinessTalkRadio, and their *Get Away for a Change* and *Professional Strategy* retreats.